This advance copy of

"DESIGN FOR GIVING"

is sent to you with

the compliments of

THE NATIONAL WAR FUND

Winthrop W. Aldrich

PRESIDENT

DESIGN FOR GIVING

EXECUTIVE COMMITTEE

Left to right: Thomas D'Arcy Brophy, Walter Rothschild, Francis
P. Matthews, Gerard Swope, J. Herbert Case, Ralph Hayes, Gordon
S. Rentschler, Mrs. Oswald B. Lord, John A. Coleman, E. A. Roberts,
Henry R. Luce, Winthrop W. Aldrich, John D. Rockefeller, Jr.,
Prescott S. Bush.

BUDGET COMMITTEE

Left to right, standing: Ralph H. Blanchard, Harold J. Seymour,
Walter S. Riepert, Elliot J. Jensen, James Brunot, Rowe S. Steel.
Seated: Ralph Hayes, Abraham Bluestein, Isidor Sack, Charles E.
Spencer, Sidney Hollander, Gerard Swope, Maxwell Hahn, Philip R.
Mather, Arthur W. Packard, S. Whitney Landon, J. Herbert Case.

Design for Giving

Giving

THE STORY OF
THE NATIONAL WAR FUND, INC.
1943-1947

HAROLD J. SEYMOUR

WITH A FOREWORD BY

WINTHROP W. ALDRICH

President, National War Fund, Inc.

HARPER & BROTHERS   NEW YORK, LONDON

CONTENTS

FOREWORD

June of 1942, six months after Pearl Harbor, was a turning point in the course of the war.

On the fighting front, the Axis powers were at high tide. In the Pacific area, we had yielded Bataan, Corregidor, Singapore, and Mandalay. In the Atlantic, the U-boats were sinking our ships by the hundreds of thousands of tons. In Africa, the British had been driven back to El Alamein, deep in Egypt. In Europe, the Germans were storming Sevastopol, and sweeping toward the Volga and Stalingrad. Dust and smoke were settling slowly over a place that once had been the little village of Lidice.

It was a time when President Roosevelt had broadcast a frank admission and a prophetic challenge:

. . . Speaking for the United States of America, let me say once and for all to the people of the world: We Americans have been compelled to yield ground, and we will regain it. We and the other United Nations are committed to the destruction of the militarism of Japan and Germany. We are daily increasing our strength. Soon we, and not our enemies, will have the offensive; we, not they, will win the final battles; and we, not they, will make the final peace.

On June 4th came the great victory of our Navy at the Battle of Midway. Later that year other events took place which foreshadowed even more clearly the ultimate Allied triumph: the British 8th Army's march to the west in Africa, the costly Canadian thrust at Dieppe, our own moves toward the attack in the Solomons and New Guinea, and then the historic landing in Africa on November 8th.

June of 1942 was also a turning point here at home.

Industry was just beginning to produce the fabulous volume of guns, ships, planes, and ammunition which later, in the hands of our Allies as well as our own, was to open the way for the V-E Day and V-J Day of 1945.

But that story, like the military and naval history, is one to be told elsewhere.

Something else happened in June of 1942; scarcely noticed at the time, but of greater long-range significance in terms of human welfare than any one of us connected with the event could possibly have foreseen.

While the Germans were sacking Lidice, a representative group of community leaders were meeting in Cincinnati. They met there, agency representatives and officers of local community chests, to discuss the problem of bringing some order out of the muddled confusion which had been brought about by the overwhelming desire of the American people to help in every possible manner to win the war—by backing up our armed forces, by sending emergency relief to the people of Allied lands, and by keeping strong our institutions here at home.

In 1940 and 1941, to hundreds of causes serving those ends, the American people had given freely and often. But by the middle of 1942, we were fairly falling over each other in a complex and undirected effort to organize, to publicize, to solicit, and to give.

Community leaders everywhere found themselves with too little time for too many causes, too little information about too many projects, and no notion whatever regarding the relative urgency of one cause as against another, or of the proper relationship between the conflicting total amounts our people were being asked to give.

Seldom had so much good will been entangled in such a mess.

Happily, those of us who were there at Cincinnati felt that World War I had already developed for us a formula for dealing with the problem of competing and conflicting appeals—the concept of cooperation through federation.

Locally, after World War I, many hundreds of communities had adopted that concept by organizing community chests, which had proved enormously successful in correlating local programs of health, welfare, and recreation agencies, and in financing them in one annual, united appeal. Significantly enough, this pattern had been initiated on the state level in 1942, in Alabama and Rhode Island.

Coming from New York City, which has no community chest, I knew all of this solely by hearsay. But as president of the British War Relief Society, and as one of many with a keen interest in the USO, and in the plight of China, Greece, France, Holland, Norway, and all the other devastated and enemy-occupied lands of our Allied neighbors, I knew very well that it was time we achieved some order and system along with our high endeavor.

I therefore proposed at that time a limited form of national federation—an Allied Relief Fund.

In the months that followed, Washington became increasingly concerned over the hundreds of new causes clamoring for official sanction, with the result that in July President Roosevelt appointed a War Relief Control Board to help bring some order out of the chaos.

The agencies met increased difficulty in finding sponsorship and support. The giving public gave, but was beginning to question the continuing confusion. The local chests were loyally bearing the burden of dozens of local budget hearings on behalf of the national agencies, and were financing as many causes as they found it possible to digest and comprehend.

As a result of all this everybody seemed to agree almost simultaneously that what was needed most was a national organization to represent the war-related agencies, the state and local groups who were being asked to organize their appeals, and the contributing public itself.

This book is the story of how that desire, arising from the grass roots and culminating in a formal request for action by President Roosevelt, resulted in the organization of the National War Fund, and of what happened in the four eventful years that followed.

Because of the interest of many thousands of those who gave the project their time and devotion to the point of genuine sacrifice, the writer has attempted to sketch briefly a story they can pleasantly remember—as a memorial to the service they rendered to help win World War II.

The main reason for the book, however, is that there are lessons from this great experience in organized cooperation to be studied and learned; both for our greater welfare here at home in the days of peace, and for the future happiness and security of our own land and of freedom-loving people everywhere.

This was a time when everyone pulled together, when these United States were a land of united people. Beyond the hundreds of millions of dollars raised, and the millions of acts of generous kindliness done as a result of a prompt and planned distribution of that money, there is a pattern here which any thoughtful American will do well to study.

WINTHROP W. ALDRICH
President, National War Fund, Inc.

I

O F F   W E   G O

In the afternoon of December 15, 1942, while Allied planes were raiding Naples, and the Germans were making their last desperate assaults at Stalingrad, six men gathered around a table in a windowless, pine-paneled conference room on the fourth floor of the home office of New York's Chase National Bank.

All they knew at the time was that the President's War Relief Control Board, aghast at the mounting confusion among hundreds of appeals to American sympathy for Allied suffering, had asked them to be an organizing committee for federating a number of war-related agencies in the interest of war-time unity and effectiveness.

What they could not have known, or probably even guessed at, was that the pebble they were going to drop that day in the broad waters of American philanthropy was to send circling ripples of effective relief and support to every corner of the world.

Certainly no one could have foreseen at that time the significant by-products of the coming effort: the organization of some 43,000 American communities in the interest of war-time unity; an increase in the number of contributors to local chests from some 16,000,000 to 20,000,000; an extension of health and welfare programs to small towns and rural communities; a sharp rise in the total number of community chests; and a war-time dividend to local home-front agencies, admittedly as a result of the deep and broad strength of the war appeal, in the form of an average budget increase of 34 per cent.

The circling ripples, it will be seen, became a rising tide. And even we native Middle Westerners know that a rising tide lifts all the boats.

So let's see now who these six men were, and what they had to talk about. For other men like them may one day have to sit in a similar meeting; for a peaceful cause, let us pray, but equally in the national interest.

Presiding, at the request of the President's War Relief Control Board, was Winthrop W. Aldrich, president of the British War Relief

1

Society, board chairman of the Chase National Bank, and an active leader in a number of major causes related to the winning of the war.

Around the table with him were Gerard Swope, of the General Electric Company, and experienced national spokesman for both community chests and the American Red Cross; Henry M. Wriston, president of Brown University, political scientist, and top man in the newly created state-wide war chest in Rhode Island; Ralph Hayes, executive director of the New York Community Trust and also vice-president of The Coca-Cola Company; and Chester I. Barnard, president of the New Jersey Bell Telephone Company, scholarly authority on management, and the on-leave full-time executive head of the USO.

These five were the committee on organization, as originally selected by the President's Board. To complete the group in the interest of recent fund-raising experience on the national level, they picked as the sixth man Prescott S. Bush, Averill Harriman's banking partner, and national campaign chairman for the successful 1942 appeal of the USO for $32,000,000.

Three points about that group of six should be noted by practicing social scientists, or by those who may wish to set up some other successful federation of national appeals to the public.

The first point is that there was nothing inside the shirts of these men but the men themselves. They were all of the type that accept committee membership with the unwritten understanding that they will attend meetings, participate actively in committee discussion, and share the load of board responsibility. Not one was there merely to "lend the use of his name."

The second point is that each in his own field had public stature, and some functional reason for being asked to serve.

And the third point, a rock on which many an effort toward unity has sadly bumped its nose, was that all were interested primarily in the total problem, and not in grinding an ax for a special interest.

There you have a picture of the men. So let's review now why they were there, and what they had to talk about.

Why they were there is in itself a long story. But the gist of it can be told quickly.

Beginning in September, 1939, when the Germans launched World War II by attacking Poland, all foreign relief appeals were required to register with the U. S. Department of State; not so much to protect American givers from duplicated or unwarranted appeals, but primarily to keep a watchful Federal eye on all matters relating to the countries involved in the war.

That this was to become a formidable kettle of a large assortment of actively struggling fish is shown by these facts: (1) that before this Federal process was finally wound up, 596 agencies for foreign relief had been registered; and (2) that these 596 agencies—by their own records—ultimately collected in the United States the tidy little sum of $597,621,366.

The original plan of registration alone may have seemed like a good idea at the time, but by the middle of 1942 the situation was just about as well in hand as a greased pig at a midnight picnic. If the Greeks have a word for madhouse, that was it.

Our country may have been neutral at the time in a military sense. But there was nothing neutral about the efforts of groups of sympathetic Americans to help sufferers overseas.

The result, as nearly everyone must remember, was that appeals were continuous, competitive, and utterly confusing; communities everywhere were running out of leadership; and—what was probably worst of all—the amount any one agency might harvest was the product of energy and emotion, rather than the result of any impartial and objective consideration of what the cause could spend effectively at the time, with due consideration for the relative urgency of other causes.

Moreover, most of the appeals were limited in geographical scope, with the result that the load was falling on major cities only, with little or no participation by the great numbers who work and live in small towns and in the country. And finally, to cap the whole sorry story, each agency had its own essential budget for fund-raising and publicity; the effect of which was to multiply costs and dissipate precious energy.

Community chests, meeting in Cincinnati in June of 1942, agreed that something ought to be done about the situation, with a degree of agreement a little startling to students of "local autonomy." The suggestion made there by Winthrop Aldrich, to the effect that all foreign appeals should be federated, was more than a seed dropped on fertile ground; the ground fairly leapt up to snatch the seed out of his hand.

By July, even the busy White House had had enough. So on July 25th, Franklin D. Roosevelt signed Executive Order 9205, taking the problem away from the State Department, and handing it to a new instrumentality which was to be known generally as "The President's War Relief Control Board."

This Board, which was to supervise and regulate, as well as merely to register agencies, included Joseph E. Davies, former Ambassador to Russia, as chairman; Charles P. Taft, Cincinnati son of William Howard, brother of Senator Taft, and a coworker of Paul McNutt's in the Federal Security Agency; and the late Frederick P. Keppel, able and dynamic president of the Carnegie Corporation of New York, who was succeeded in 1943 by Charles Warren, historian and former Assistant Attorney General.

Meanwhile, the national chest body, Community Chests and Councils, Inc., was sounding the alarms in a big way, urging local community chests forthwith to become local war chests, so that the appeals usually made in October could embrace some portion of the total war-related problem, as well as the usual appeals for local home-front agencies.

At the same time, the national chest organization, immediately following the Cincinnati meeting, appointed national committees to deal with two of the most pressing and difficult problems—problems that could be approached only on some national basis.

The first, the problem of budget review for war-related agencies wishing to be included in local war chests, was referred to a representative budget committee, under the leadership of Gerard Swope. This committee recommended to local chests agency budgets of some $76,000,000, of which some $59,000,000 was locally accepted.

The other, the problem of how much any given community should be asked to give, with relation to amounts sought in other communities, was assigned to a national quota committee, headed by Harry Wareham, executive director of the local chest in Rochester, New York. This committee, after casting up 15 economic factors, which previously had been tried out in a regional study in southern California, brought out recommended state percentages of quota participation, but wisely left the question of local percentages to be decided within the respective states.   .

Here, then, by the Fall of 1942, were all the grass-roots elements for creating a national chest for war-related appeals: local demand, official demand in Washington, efforts toward clarity by the national body representing local chests, dissatisfaction among many of the agencies, and incidentally, increasing pressure from the Treasury and the Office of War Information to keep the decks clear during longer periods of the year for war-bond drives and other promotional efforts essential to the military conduct of the war.

The general scramble simply had to stop. Late that Fall, the President's Board asked Mr. Aldrich and the four other men to set up some new organization—to end the confusion, but to keep the warm stream of American aid and sympathy flowing more strongly than ever, in channels of orderly effectiveness.

That, then, perhaps not as briefly as you were cheerfully promised some paragraphs ago, is why the men were there on that afternoon of December 15, 1942.

What they had to talk about was plenty, as by this time anyone can easily guess.

"What agencies should be included? How much do they need? How much can be raised? When should we make the appeal, and how can the agencies be financed in the meanwhile? How are we going to organize, so that every community in the United States can participate? What does experience show? How are we going to finance the preliminary expense? What are we going to call this organization? Where is the staff coming from?"

These and a number of similar questions fairly swarmed around the table.

One thing, however, was clear to the group; namely, that the first requirement was a set of rules for the game—a framework of basic policy within which the other questions could be taken up in an orderly and logical way.

That framework was not drafted overnight. It developed. But to understand the story as it unfolded in the next three years, and to see the guideposts which others may wish to find at some later day, perhaps the next section of this recital should side-step many of the preliminary moves, and get right into policy.

These policies were not pronunciamentos from an Ivory Tower; they were in every case, in a real sense, the practical application of grassroots experience to a situation in which none of the parties at interest could possibly get all they asked for, but in which everyone had to be reasonably satisfied.

Effective cooperation, it was to be found, always necessitates some sacrifice of self-interest.

II

RULES OF THE GAME

Phrase-making Patrick Henry once said, "I have but one lamp by which my feet are guided, and that is the lamp of experience."

We could have used a good lamp of that sort in December, 1942. There was plenty of experience available among the individual war-related agencies, some of which had been conducting their own individual appeals for two or three years. There was also available a wealth of experience on the federation of agencies in local communities. Only in the memories of a few, however, was there anything to be found about the last united war appeal in World War I.

Newspaper files disclosed that this previous united cause was launched right after the Armistice of November 11, 1918, and that a grateful and joyous people had quickly contributed more than $200,000,000. Beyond that, and the fact that several veterans of the effort recalled happily that the money was raised with hardly any trouble at all, inquiry drew a blank. It was "just a breeze," and a breeze that left scarcely any more trace behind it than a zephyr off a country pond.

That, incidentally, is the main reason for this chronicle of ours; so that next time, if there is to be a next time, some record can be found for what was done between December 15, 1942, and December 31, 1946 —the period of the active life of the National War Fund.

Starting virtually from scratch, then, as the organizing committee was thus obliged to do, orderly procedure alone dictated that they should first of all define the proposed effort, in terms of purpose and scope.

PURPOSE AND SCOPE

Defining the purpose was relatively simple. It was decided with little or no debate that "the National War Fund is a philanthropic federation with three simple aims; first, to determine the nature and the extent of the war-related needs; second, to see that everybody has

6

a chance to contribute to the funds required; and third, to channel the sums raised for its member agencies wherever American help is currently most needed—enough and on time."

Defining the scope of the Fund, however, was not quite so easy.

Literally hundreds of foreign relief agencies were registered at the time with the President's War Relief Control Board. Who was to say which agencies should be included in the Fund?

Foreign relief, in turn, was only one facet of the problem. There were prisoners of war to be considered, our own merchant seamen, and refugees whose plight crossed frontiers and who therefore were outside the province of agencies having to do with one particular country only. Most important, in popular interest and in size of budget, was the USO—which for two years had successfully financed itself in nation-wide campaigns, and which least of all needed help from the new federation.

There was also a problem in what to do about agencies which many of the churches had organized. Theirs were appeals to their own special constituencies. Question: Should any of these denominational groups be included, and if so, on what basis?

Hottest question of all, as events turned out, was what to do about the relief programs of the American Federation of Labor and the C. I. O. Here were two great labor bodies, each prepared after long planning and field work to launch their own drives among union members, for relief to union members in other lands. There was nothing new about this, as organized labor had had such programs for more than fifty years. But it was plain that any such separate campaigns, particularly in light of the fact that each planned to ask employers to contribute too, would cut straight across any one united effort, and would add more confusion to an already badly tangled situation.

All these questions, coupled with the obvious fact that there was some practical limit to the amount of money that could be raised in one united appeal, gave rise by degrees to the Fund's "policy on inclusion." And that settled the puzzling question of defining the Fund's scope.

POLICY ON INCLUSION

First, as a measure of preliminary screening, it was determined that no agency would be admitted to the Fund unless it had been certified for membership by the President's Board. This solved a large part of the membership problem, as the Board certified an agency only after checking its program and proposed budget with the State Department, the American Red Cross, sometimes the War Department, and often other Government agencies controlling export licenses, priorities in the purchase of supplies, and the like. Certification thus implied avoidance of duplication of effort, and clearance on diplomatic, military, and economic levels.

Second, it was determined that the Fund would include only one agency for any given country or function. This was easy of accomplishment as far as service to our own forces was concerned, as the USO and United Seamen's Service were the only agencies with the official status of serving the Army, the Navy, and our merchant seamen, in ways not duplicated by the American Red Cross. Similarly, no other agency was in the field of the U. S. Committee for the Care of European Children.

Otherwise, the policy necessitated a move which was clearly in the public interest, but which otherwise might never have been brought about; namely, the consolidation of agencies with comparable objectives.

Three agencies in the refugee field were thus brought together as "Refugee Relief Trustees." Similarly, when it was found that War Relief Services of the National Catholic Welfare Conference was contemplating a program for prisoners of war, it was necessary to set up a new instrumentality called "War Prisoners Aid, Inc.," through which the Fund could channel aid both to the Catholic program and to the long-established committee of the international Y. M. C. A.

The problem of nationality agencies, however, was not so simple. Friends of China had solved the problem back in 1941, by federating eight American agencies in a new organization called "United China Relief." Friends of Britain had also solved the problem by banding together 13 agencies as the British War Relief Society. Russian War Relief was also in a position of acting as the only officially recognized American agency for sending relief to the people of the Soviet Union.

Otherwise, the President's Board had a tough nut to crack. There were two big agencies appealing for France, with the respective leaders not seeing eye to eye, to put it mildly, on the subject of contemporary French politics. Let us say merely that some little negotiation was necessitated in order to combine these and other agencies for France in one united organization—"American Relief for France."

But eventually, this process of consolidation was successfully consummated for all the countries concerned, with the single exception of Yugoslavia. Not all the powers of the President's Board, nor all the king's horses and all the king's men, were ever able to resolve the fundamental cleavage between the political sympathies of the two main groups of Americans of Yugoslav sympathies or descent.

Third, it was decided that the National War Fund could serve no special interest; that its appeal had to be confined to causes which all Americans could be asked to support.

This meant that all the money contributed through the instrumentality of the National War Fund had to be disbursed without regard to color, creed, race, or political affiliation. Specifically, it meant that labor-sponsored projects could not be designed for the relief of labor groups alone, and that no denominational relief program, to the extent that it was financed by the National War Fund, could confine its work to the adherents of its own faith.

That seemed clear enough, and met with no serious objection from anyone. But it still left unsolved the problem of public interpretation; how to identify the agencies of the Fund in such a way as to leave no doubt about the practical implementation of policy.

Just as we would have welcomed the participation of any other important religious group, everyone wanted to include the Catholic agency, both in the interest of unity and for the practical reason that the world-wide organization of the Roman Catholic Church, and the long experience of its priests and sisterhoods in the field of charity, provided a ready channel for speedy, effective, and economical relief. But everyone also recognized that to list such an agency without policy explanation—something obviously impossible in a mere list—would be to invite question and confusion.

Similarly, it was recognized that there could be no united effort without organized labor, and that the labor-sponsored projects, which had been initiated previously with community chest support, could not fairly be set aside. But labor's own leaders were quick to see that the unexplained listing of the labor committees as member agencies of the Fund would make a swarm of angry hornets seem like a herd of contented cows.

So we fell back on our semantics.

First, we classified as "member agencies" all those agencies whose purpose fell within one clearly defined function or geographical entity; the USO for service to our own armed forces, United Seamen's Service for our own merchant marine, the British War Relief Society for Britain, Greek War Relief Association for Greece, and so on.

Second, we grouped as "participating services" those agencies which were to operate their own programs, and to be financed by the Fund, but whose scope crossed the boundary lines of more than one of the United Nations. The National War Fund made direct remittances to none of these services. Instead, remittances were channeled to them through the member agencies. The British War Relief Society, for example, would act as the channel for remittances from the Fund for the Catholic program in Malta, and for the program of the World Emergency and War Victims Fund of the Y. W. C. A. in Egypt.

Third, we classified the two relief committees of organized labor as "cooperating organizations," for the reason that neither fell in either of the other two categories. Neither of the labor committees was constituted as an operating relief agency, with the result that neither handled any of the relief remittances of the National War Fund at any time. Labor merely sponsored certain relief projects in certain countries, which their committees could interpret to the ranks of organized labor as projects in which labor had a particular interest. Funds for the projects, in every case, were channeled through the member agencies for the countries concerned, and subject to their administrative supervision.

Fourth, and finally, the policy of inclusion left to the National War Fund itself the final judgment on whether or not any given agency was to be included. No agency not certified by the President's War Relief Control Board could be included, but certification in itself was not grounds enough for inclusion. Under this phase of policy, the Fund in its later stages was to decline admittance to American Relief for India, on the ground of greater urgency in countries which had suffered the full effects of enemy occupation. Likewise, after V-E Day, the Fund was to take the position that it could not recognize new agencies for relief in ex-enemy countries.

The net effect of these four phases of the policy on inclusion was to force the maximum degree of amalgamation and unity among the relief agencies, to eliminate virtually all of the problem of duplication in agency programs, and to enable the National War Fund to present an appeal which could be truly characterized as "for our own—for our Allies."

At any rate, this settled the question of who was going to belong to the new organization. And that led naturally to the next broad policy question—"What kind of an organization was the Fund to be?"

POLICY ON ORGANIZATION

As a new and temporary organization, the National War Fund, like a Missouri mule, had neither pride of ancestry nor hope of posterity. It was free, therefore, to fashion its own design without restrictions of precedent, and with an eye solely to its war-related tenure.

The policy on organization comprised five simple fundamentals.

First, it was made clear from the outset that the Fund represented no single interest, or group of interests, but literally everyone. After the Fund had been operating for more than a year, this phase of policy was outlined to the Board of Directors by President Aldrich in these words:

We represent the member agencies, and we intend to represent them honestly and vigorously; not only as their fund-raising agent, but as the champion of the great causes they serve. But we also represent the American people, through their state and local funds, and we intend to represent them fairly and reasonably; not only in distributing the fruits of their past generosity, but in determining how much, under all the existing circumstances, they should be asked to contribute.

Initially, in the organization stage, the most important application of this principle was in choosing members for the Executive Committee and the Board on the basis of broad interest rather than direct representation of specific agencies. In this and in every other possible way, the Fund sought to keep itself in the position of representing the total interest of all parties concerned, with the single objective of helping to win the war.

Second, the organization was based on a primary acceptance of the principle of full and dynamic federation.

For the sake of war-time unity, and conservation of effort and cost, the Fund was ready to associate its appeal with all community chests, and in other communities with federated efforts of a similar kind. In a town with no community chest, for example, the responsible local leaders could, if they so wished, establish a local war fund by adding to the quota for the National War Fund other budgets for purely local purposes; such as a fund for visiting nurse services, a fund for the Boy Scouts, and so on. (Many a town did just that, with the immediate result that social services were introduced for the first time, and with the later result of creating many a new community chest.)

But the Fund also insisted that federation be dynamic, with full

acceptance of a fair assignment of responsibility all along the line—
nationally, in all the states, and in every community.

The reason that is worth stressing is that federation doesn't always
work that way. Sometimes it can function merely as a defense mechanism—either a sort of Chinese Wall for the protection of reluctant
givers, or else a protective huddling together of otherwise impotent
forces, like so many sheep in a storm. Such types of federation lead
from weakness, whereas the National War Fund sought to lead from
strength; from a belief in the justice of its related causes, and from
faith that every community would respond generously with its fair
share of the total load.

Third, the organization was designed on the principle of maximum
decentralization.

One of the first thoughts that should occur to any group planning
to set up a new national organization is that Kearny, Nebraska, many
miles west of Omaha, is just halfway between Boston and San Francisco; in short, that ours is a very big country. Maine likes things one
way, and Texas another way. No national pattern of suggested procedure, therefore, can amount to much more than a guide for local
discussion.

In its practical application, this phase of the policy on organization
meant that all of the functions involved in the operation of the National
War Fund were clearly defined on three levels—national, state, and
local—and that each level was expected to exercise fully the functions
that were theirs.

How this worked out will be seen later; the emphasis here, for its
value to others, should be on the principle—maximum decentralization, with each echelon of function clearly defined and fully exercised.

Fourth, the organization was set up on a foundation of mutual
understanding and goodwill, rather than on a legalistic basis of binding
contracts.

Agreements were executed, to be sure, between the Fund and the
agencies, and between the Fund and all the state organizations. But
these were primarily for the purpose of insuring mutual understanding,
and not for the sake of attempting to bind anyone legally. And this
was not sheer benevolence; experience was to prove that understanding
and goodwill were paramount, and that contracts in themselves were
scarcely worth their ink and paper.

Fifth, and finally, the policy on organization called for the fullest
possible exercise of simplicity and economy. And as you will find when

we get to the operating story, the exercise of this phase of policy resulted in quite a bit done by very few, at a cost that never drew criticism.

The essence of these five phases of the policy on organization was that the National War Fund was built on the structure of what Chester I. Barnard calls authoritative advice, rather than authoritarian control; that the Fund was designed, and was operated, as a voluntary, nation-wide project in the area of public relations.

POLICY ON BUDGETING

It is in the nature of things, in any federation of agencies, that the total amount of money the agencies would like to have is always materially more than the amount it is possible to raise. Even within the amount that can be allocated, no agency, as a general rule, is ever content with its allotted portion.

This is not a matter of insatiable institutional appetite; on the contrary, it is sound evidence that the agencies are on their toes, with sound and defensible plans for projected useful service.

But it does pose a problem for budget committees.

The budget committee of the National War Fund was faced by this universal budget problem, and by several other problems inherent in the particular situation.

First of all, it was confronted by 22 member agencies in widely varying degrees of solvency; some had substantial funds and pledges in hand, some very little or none.

Second, bearing in mind that the chief purpose of the Fund was to help to win the war, the committee was obliged to take counsel with those who were running our part in the war; namely, a number of men with key posts in Washington.

Third, they had to take into account the fact that the tides of war were subject to swift change; that a relief program in one country might have to step aside quickly in the interest of a newly liberated area.

And finally, they had to provide for fund-raising purposes, despite the dangers of long-term implied commitments, an immediate schedule of allocations to all agencies for the period to be covered by any given campaign, so that prospective contributors could see what the Fund proposed to do with their money.

All of this necessitated a framework of policy for budgeting, in six main phases.

The only possible answer to the wide variation in the financial status of the agencies, at the time they came into the Fund, was to decide as a matter of policy that payments to agencies were to be supplementary only, as deficit financing. As an essential corollary, agencies were not to be allowed to carry forward any unspent balances at the end of a budget year.

In light of the fact that fund-raising campaigns for the Fund were held in most communities some eight months after the Fund was organized, this policy played a major role in handling the financing of the agencies during the difficult first year.

As it was, the Fund was obliged to borrow $17,500,000 from a nation-wide group of banks; a sum which would have been far from sufficient if some of the agencies had not come into the Fund with substantial resources of their own—resources collected in the previous year, and which they had not yet been able to spend effectively because of conditions currently imposed by the course of the war.

The second phase of the policy on budgeting had to do with the always troublesome question of how far the Fund's budget committee should go in passing upon specific projects in agency programs.

Dr. Wriston and others with local community chest backgrounds took the unequivocal position that financing should be kept clear of program; that interference with agency planning by the fund-raising instrumentality was a sure way to wreck a federation. Yet the Fund had to be in a position to give certain assurances to the contributing public.

The decision, in terms of policy, was that the budget committee subjected agency projects to one general question—"Will this help win the war or help win lasting peace?" And that is one of the principal reasons why the Fund insisted upon Washington approval of all agency projects before they were permitted to come before the budget committee.

Another reason for close Washington liaison was concerned with the third phase of budget policy; namely, that no funds raised by voluntary contribution should be spent for purposes for which public funds were available. If relief could be extended through Lend-Lease, then no private funds should be spent in the same area. Private funds, it was held, should be confined to emergency situations for which no public funds could be found.

On no point of policy was there so little disagreement, and yet so much confusion.

One of the largest red herrings ever drawn across anyone's path was the period of preliminary publicity for UNRRA, in the late Fall of 1943. On the face of it, the United Nations Relief and Rehabilitation Administration was quickly going to spend billions for what most people thought was "relief." So why a few paltry millions for relief through the National War Fund? The United States will be the biggest of the UNRRA underwriters, and we'll all have to pay for it through taxes. So why give twice for the same thing?

Of course, except during the final phases of the UNRRA operation, it never was the same thing, and the word "relief" never should have been included in the UNRRA name. But once those original UNRRA stories started making page one in the daily press, the task of the National War Fund was doubly difficult. Fast and accurate interpretation was all that saved the day for the Fund's relief appeal during the latter weeks of 1943, but some degree of confusion persisted for two more years.

The moral for the future is that function should always be defined clearly and sharply; that a tent that tries to cover too much ground is apt to fall down when the wind starts to blow.

The fourth phase of the Fund's budget policy was an insistence on maximum elasticity in allocations to agencies. For campaign purposes, it was essential to start the year with a tentative total for each agency; always coupled, however, with a public explanation that all budgets were subject to quarterly review.

This made it possible to shift the emphasis of the Fund's relief appropriation with shifts in the course of the war; stepping up the budget quickly for a country newly liberated, reducing one program in the interest of another more urgent, and toward the end, swinging the major force of the Fund's help to those countries which were the last to be freed.

Incidentally, a quarterly review was as fast as the budget process could possibly move. It took virtually the entire three months, it was found, to go through the painstaking cycle: program preparation by the agencies; budget interpretation on the standard forms required by the Fund; preliminary consultation by staff; consolidation of all budget requests by the Fund's budget department; review and report by Washington; revision in light of Washington comment; advance distribution of full information for members of the budget committee; the two days of formal budget hearings; and finally, the notification of action to all the agencies. By the time all this had taken place, it was time to start the process all over again.

The fifth phase of budget policy had to do with the composition and operation of the budget committee itself; the policy being to insure the maximum degree of quality of judgment and continuity of information.

The chairman himself, Gerard Swope, was chosen not alone for his seasoned judgment and fairness, but also because of his experience in 1942 as chairman of the budget committee of Community Chests and Councils, Inc. With him, at the outset, was a nucleus of men who had also served on that committee. Additions were made on the basis of long experience in reviewing agency programs; chiefly among local chests and the philanthropic foundations. The result was that the budget committee comprised, as it should, men of broad sympathy for the common ends in view, but who also had had long training in studying budgets with impartial objectivity.

For continuity of information, the committee was divided into three or more panels, each of which met with the same agencies from one hearing to another, and in that way acquired a long-term background of agency purpose against which to judge the particular projects under current review.

Finally, the sixth phase of budget policy was that full information on agency programs and budgets should be made available to everyone. In the Fund's first year, this policy was carried to the point of publishing a "budget book," sent to all state and local war fund organizations. Interestingly enough, the book's welcome was tempered in many communities by the embarrassing circumstances that no comparable report was available on the chest's own local agencies. We published no "budget book" in the two succeeding years, but continued to supply detailed information about the agencies in a "case book," designed generally as a source book for local publicity programs.

These, then, were the six main phases of policy on budgeting; the total effect of which, if not leading to contentment, at least gave rise to no serious complaint. And in the budget field, as any budgeter can tell you, absence of serious complaint is equivalent to unqualified praise.

POLICY ON FUND-RAISING

Money is always raised locally; all you can do nationally is to try to persuade all local communities to run campaigns for a common purpose, at substantially the same time.

This is no mere nice distinction. On the contrary, it is the fundamental fact, not always readily understood, which controls all policy and operation.

Many think, for example, that the goal of a national campaign for a federation of related causes, such as the National War Fund, is or should be determined by adding up all the requested agency budgets, together with an allowance for costs, and deciding that that is the needed amount, and therefore the goal.

That is not the way it works.

One of the first problems of the National War Fund, for example, was to decide how much local campaigns should be asked to raise; knowing full well, in advance of budget hearings, that the need for relief was virtually unlimited, and that the USO alone would probably require at least $60,000,000.

There were two sets of known factors; first, how much each agency had raised by its own effort in 1942, and second, what proportion of any national goal was ordinarily taken by a number of local communities.

We knew, for example, that in 1942 the USO had raised $33,000,000 on a budget of $32,000,000, that the British War Relief Society had raised $3,873,728, United China Relief $6,885,169, and Russian War Relief—in 15 months ending December 31, 1942—$6,502,478.

We knew too that Cincinnati, for example, ordinarily assumed the responsibility for one per cent of any national goal, Cleveland two per cent, Rochester three-quarters of one per cent, and so on.

The first set of factors established a floor for the goal, for the reason that the Fund could hardly propose to raise for the agencies any less than the total of what they had raised alone. The second set of factors established the ceiling, for the equally practical reason that we could not ask any community to increase its total local goal to the point of probable failure; the total local goal involving budgets for established local agencies as well as the local quota for the National War Fund.

The effect of approaching the question of campaign goal in light of all these factors was to establish the initial policy on fund-raising; namely, to ask for all the traffic would bear.

In the first year, then, with one eye on the unlimited need, and the other eye on the fact that Cincinnati's quota, for instance, would be substantially more than a million dollars, the goal was expressed nationally as a total of $125,000,000. Actually, for the reason again that there is no such thing as a national campaign, there was no national goal. We established $125,000,000 as a national budget, with the goal always expressed locally in terms of the total federated objective in each community.

Other policies on fund-raising were either clarifications of the principles of unity and federation, or practical applications of the principles of decentralization and local autonomy.

For one thing, it was established from the outset that the budget of the Fund was no table d'hôte menu, from which chests or contributors could pick selections of favored agencies. The menu was strictly on the American plan, with one price, in terms of quota, for the whole list. No other plan would have given validity to the actions of the Fund's budget committee. And any selective basis would have led to a log-rolling performance that would have made the fabled Paul Bunyan look like an invalid playing with matches. The policy, then, was to sell one united package—take one, take all.

The next question was one of quotas; how to determine how much any one community should be asked to give. The policy here was that the national quota system should go no further than to allot a certain percentage of $125,000,000 to each of the 48 states and the District of Columbia; leaving it to the states, in turn, to decide by their own processes what the quotas should be for counties and local communities. To be sure, we furnished each state with suggested county quotas, but the decision and the discussion was left solely in state hands.

If anyone should ever compile a list of one hundred ways in which to keep out of serious trouble in so-called national campaigns, this policy alone should stand close to the top. For as we said before, this is indeed a big country, and the greater the distance from which a local wound is inflicted the more freely it always bleeds.

Another question, never solved with satisfaction all around, was what to do about campaign failures and oversubscriptions. In chest cities, the local quota of the National War Fund was to go into partnership, in effect, with a number of permanent local agencies on one united appeal. Should they share and share alike, for better or for worse? Or should the permanent local agencies be protected in some way, in the event that significant campaign failure should imperil essential health and welfare services here at home? Furthermore, if a given community should meet its National War Fund quota in full, why wouldn't that be enough?

Nationally, we thought we had good answers to all such questions. The war services too were essential, and unless we could share in oversubscriptions it was obvious that the Fund would be sure to fail by the total amount of failure locally.

The national policy, therefore, as expressed in the standard agreement between the Fund and the state organizations, was that after deducting necessary expense, all moneys raised for or in the name of the Fund should be sent by states to the Fund; the understanding being that the states in turn would seek to negotiate local agreements in which oversubscriptions should be shared proportionately.

Unhappily, on the more troublesome question of possible undersubscription, it was felt necessary to compromise. This led to the so-called "95 per cent clause," which meant that if local chest campaigns reached 95 per cent of their goals, the campaign proceeds would be shared proportionately between the local agencies and the Fund; but that if failure exceeded 5 per cent, the Fund would take the brunt of the loss.

This was a technicality in 1943 and 1944, when local campaigns almost everywhere attained their full goals. But the year 1945 was to prove that the clause was a lethal weapon from the point of view of the war-related agencies. In that final year, after V-J Day, and with the national economy already beginning its dizzy dance with abnormalcy, campaign failures of 10 per cent frequently cost the Fund as much as 30 per cent of local quotas. That was when we all lent extra fervor to our prayers of thanks for the good stout states, like the state of Michigan, in which, from the very first, all chests played the game on a share-and-share-alike basis. At any rate, let those who may one day follow in the steps of the National War Fund be warned that one of the principal Jabberwockies of which to beware is the "95 per cent clause." Share-and-share-alike is the ideal; at a minimum to the extent of a 10 per cent local failure.

The rest of fund-raising policy may be interesting, but is hardly so controversial.

In keeping with decentralization, we suggested method, but never sought to impose it. In line with good practice locally, we frowned upon most schemes for raising money by "benefits," and on all schemes for street collections, tag days, shaking boxes and cans for shoeshine money, and tying the Fund's appeal to other types of promotion.

Nationally, in order to preserve the unity of community campaigns, we solicited very few gifts; less than 85 national contributions each year. No solicitation was conducted nationally without the consent of the local community in which the person or corporation maintained principal residence or home office, and all solicitation was confined to two general classes of prospective contributors: either those whose gifts would help establish a high standard of giving, or those to whom a purely local approach was thought to be relatively less promising.

Similarly, to preserve local unity, we approved no plans which might have cut across community lines, such as any nationally sponsored solicitation of members of a fraternal order or patriotic society, and consistently warned all fund-raising units against adopting any plan of fund-raising contrary to the principle of proportionate giving—such as "buck a month clubs," or any other version of the "March of Dimes" idea. The principle here is that everyone should have equal opportunity to give, but that everyone should give in proportion to his available means; a principle always basic to maximum results at minimum cost and effort.

And finally, recognizing again that campaigns are always run locally, how and when the local leaders may decide, the national policy on timing was to set a date on which campaigns were supposed to start, and on which the President of the United States would in fact start the national publicity program by a White House broadcast—but to say nothing at all about any date for closing, and never to announce a national result until many months later. For just as the sun never sets on the British flag, the seasons never close on community campaigns.

POLICY ON PUBLIC RELATIONS

Most people are just now coming to realize that public relations, fundamentally, are nothing more than good manners; the art of dealing with others as you prefer to be dealt with yourself.

With little or no real authority, and with virtually all its operations dependent on good will, the National War Fund in all its aspects was essentially a public relations operation. Its entire framework of policy, therefore, might well be characterized as public relations policy.

For that reason, there is little to be cited for the record as policy under the heading of public relations as such.

Probably of most importance, toward the end of winning public confidence and acceptance, was the policy that the Fund had no secrets. By deliberate intent, it lived in a goldfish bowl; telling everything, concealing nothing, always ready to try to answer any question.

Another policy worth recording, as a means of achieving both economy and good relations, was the policy of minding our own business.

The Fund restricted its own publicity operations to the affairs of the Fund itself; letting the agencies interpret their own programs, and putting it up to all state and local war funds to publicize their own activities. Except in the areas that had to be covered nationally, such as radio networks and national magazines, the Fund's publicity operations were designed not to obtain maximum national publicity, but rather to serve state and local publicity committees in such a way as to get maximum publicity for community campaigns. We never tried to make records; we merely sought to make friends.

Like the little drops of water and the little grains of sand, any successful program of public relations is the sum total of a multitude of little things. Expressed in terms of policy, the National War Fund sought to indoctrinate all of its personnel on the importance of "the tremendous trifles"; writing a man's name the way he wants it written, answering all mail promptly and cheerfully, using good manners over the telephone, never being too busy to see visitors, always keeping the door open on every office, and above almost all, never letting it be said that "Mr. Doakes is in conference."

Finally, the Fund always sought to distinguish sharply between its own importance and the importance of its task.

The task we took seriously indeed. We constantly stressed its importance, and tried our best to win general agreement that it was a vital task, meriting prompt, generous, and universal support.

The Fund itself (meaning, of course, the people in it) we regarded in a wholly different light. From Winthrop W. Aldrich, president of the Fund, to Charle Broach, genial head messenger, everyone tried to do well what they were supposed to do, and a little more too; but no one suffered from any Atlas complex, in the belief that our shoulders, and ours alone, could support the weight of a world's burdens.

The spirit, in short, was akin to what must have been in the mind of General Eisenhower when someone asked him who won the war.

"Those," he said, "who did what they could."

III

BACK TO THE GRASS ROOTS

Now we come to dynamics; how the National War Fund grew in a few months from six men and an idea to an enterprise doing a business of more than a hundred million dollars a year, with active representatives in 43,000 communities.

It was just the reverse of the magician's pet phrase. In this case, it was "Now you don't see it, and now you do." And much of it seems just a bit fabulous, as one looks back.

Perhaps the best way to tell the story, as a pattern for those who might wish to organize a similar undertaking, is to describe what happened on two successive levels—national and state.

NATIONAL ORGANIZATION

Nationally, we started with six men and an idea. There was no corporation, no staff, no office, no plan, no money. If there is really an advantage in getting off to a clean start, then the National War Fund started under the happiest of auspices.

Incorporation, in the experienced hands of Sullivan and Cromwell, Counsel, was a relatively simple matter, under the laws of the State of New York governing membership corporations. Not so simple, however, was the question of how to make the Fund a democratic and representative body, and at the same time insure swift and responsible action. We wanted something that looked like a calliope with 48 keyboards. But we knew too that once in a while it might have to resemble a self-starting steam roller.

The legal result, as all bright readers have guessed, was a compromise. The members of the corporation were the six members of the organizing committee; with full powers, under the bylaws, to appoint or elect committees and members of the board, to formulate policy, and in short, to do anything at all within the distant limits of the Fund's broad charter.* But at the same time, provision was made for

* See Appendix A.

22

a large and representative board of directors, with an executive committee empowered to handle all interim business.

In practice, the members merely held a *pro forma* annual meeting, and served as a nominating committee for the election of officers at the annual meeting of the board. All the business was done by the executive committee.

In selecting the original members of the board, the primary consideration was to insure proportionate representation among the three major faiths, labor and management, the interests served by the agencies, and the state organizations to be responsible for organizing community campaigns.

It was thought, at first, that this end could be reached by a board of 75 members. Later, we were obliged to change the bylaws four times, in order to accommodate the eventual membership of 175. One of the reasons for this, it should be noted, was that all state war fund presidents were exofficio members of the national board. As the states changed officers, in the course of the three years, usual practice would have indicated that membership on the national board should have changed accordingly. Knowing the organization to be temporary, however, and needing maximum state representation for quorums and for influence, we made no such changes. So like Topsy, the board just grew.

Under the restriction of war-time travel, meetings of the board were necessarily restricted. In all, during the three active years of the Fund, there were six meetings, all held in New York City.

The executive committee, as a rule, met at monthly intervals, with the minutes of each meeting mailed to all members of the board. The budget committee usually met at quarterly intervals, though special panels were called together on a number of emergency occasions. The public relations committee, responsible for the planning and production of national promotional material, held no meetings at stated times; it met and functioned as long in advance of the annual appeal as was practically feasible, and continued its meetings until its annual task was finished.

On the campaign side of the national setup, under Prescott S. Bush, National Campaign Chairman, there were three committees: a Committee on National Corporations, the Special Services Committee, and the Quota Review Committee.

The Committee on National Corporations, headed in 1943 and 1944 by Irving S. Olds, Chairman of the Board of the United States

Steel Corporation, and in 1945 by Edward L. Ryerson, Chairman of the Board of the Inland Steel Company, was responsible for the solicitation of less than 100 national corporations. It usually met in May, to adopt the program for the year, and thereafter functioned without formal meetings, on the basis of individual assignments to five or six committee members.

The Special Services Committee, headed by Terrance L. Webster, Executive Director of the Community Chest of Columbus and Franklin County, comprised a representative group of community chest executives, and met several times a year to discuss a number of technical campaign problems, such as the solicitation of corporate gifts, persuading a greater number of national corporations to permit payroll deductions on gifts by employees, ways in which official Washington could be of assistance to local campaigns, techniques for increasing the support of organized labor, and kindred matters. Though comprised almost wholly of professional people, this committee served as a lay committee.

The Quota Review Committee, headed first by J. Cameron Thomson of Minnesota, and later by Charles A. Russell, President of The Edward W. Hazen Foundation, Inc., Haddam, Connecticut, served as a court of review for any questions raised by state committees on the quotas assigned to states. It met only when there was business to be done, and that was happily seldom.

The Advisory Cabinet, headed by C. M. Bookman, Executive Vice-President of the Community Chest of Cincinnati and Hamilton County, served as occasional counsel to the administration of the Fund; mostly on problems having to do with the campaign, but without any limitation of function. Comprising at each meeting some 15 or 20 of the leading community chest executives in the country, this cabinet was helpful both in the formulation of policy and in obtaining leadership in the entire community chest movement for measures in the interest of the Fund. Though wholly a professional group, this committee too served as a lay committee.

The original national staff, almost to a man, was simply commandeered.

The problems of chest relationships, and relationships with agencies, called for executives with community chest experience. As executive vice-presidents, therefore, the Fund arranged for the services of Harry P. Wareham of Rochester and Robert O. Loosley of Providence; each of whom served full-time during the organizing period, and then took

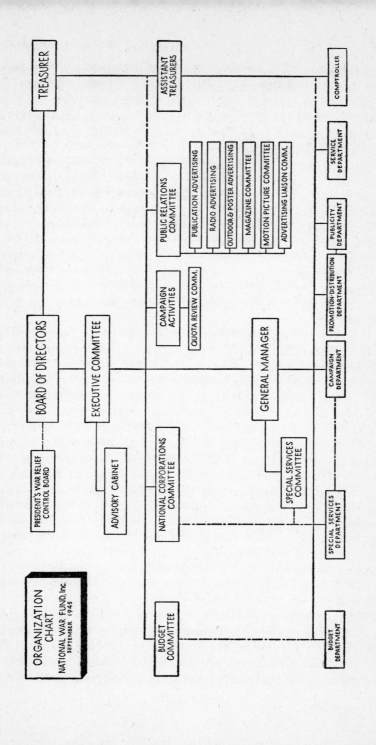

ORGANIZATION CHART
NATIONAL WAR FUND, Inc.
SEPTEMBER 1945

TREASURER

ASSISTANT TREASURERS

COMPTROLLER

BOARD OF DIRECTORS

PRESIDENT'S WAR RELIEF CONTROL BOARD

EXECUTIVE COMMITTEE

ADVISORY CABINET

CAMPAIGN ACTIVITIES

QUOTA REVIEW COMM.

PUBLIC RELATIONS COMMITTEE

PUBLICATION ADVERTISING
RADIO ADVERTISING
OUTDOOR & POSTER ADVERTISING
MAGAZINE COMMITTEE
MOTION PICTURE COMMITTEE
ADVERTISING LIAISON COMM.

NATIONAL CORPORATIONS COMMITTEE

GENERAL MANAGER

SPECIAL SERVICES COMMITTEE

BUDGET COMMITTEE

SPECIAL SERVICES DEPARTMENT

BUDGET DEPARTMENT

CAMPAIGN DEPARTMENT

PROMOTION-DISTRIBUTION DEPARTMENT

PUBLICITY DEPARTMENT

SERVICE DEPARTMENT

turns at the office while the other was at home running his own local chest campaign. Neither, in fairness to his primary responsibility to his own local chest, was able to continue this leave of absence arrangement beyond the Fund's critical first year.

Also representing the chest movement, among the original staff, were four men commandeered from Community Chests and Councils, Inc.: Allen T. Burns, retiring executive director, who served for a short time as secretary of the budget committee; Virgil Martin, newly appointed director of the campaign department of the national chest organization, and who arrived from Indianapolis only to find that he had been drafted by the Fund as head of its Special Services division; Bent Taylor, national chest publicity chief, who was called to the Fund to represent the chest interests in publicity and promotion; and Ralph H. Blanchard, newly elected executive director of Community Chests and Councils, Inc., who served the Fund throughout as chief friend and counsellor for the management, and, after the first year, as secretary of the board of directors.

But the Fund also needed staff people with experience in national fund-raising. For that purpose, it could have drawn on the staffs of a number of the member agencies, each of which was now to abandon independent fund-raising. It seemed simpler, however, merely to take over the campaign staff of the USO, which had worked together as a team for two years, and which in 1942 had established more local campaigns than any other war-related agency. (It was for this reason— to introduce a personal note essential for clarification—that I was originally engaged as campaign manager; becoming general manager of the Fund late in 1943.)

Finally, staff was needed on the accounting side of the operation. And here the Fund was able, fortunately, to draw on the National City Bank and the auditors, Price, Waterhouse & Company. The bank furnished the full-time services of Leo Chamberlain, a veteran of their Far Eastern service, who had just been released from a Jap concentration camp, as Comptroller, and also furnished the part-time services of several officers, each of whom served from time to time as an Assistant Treasurer; H. O. Westmen, Robert E. Pearce, A. Halsey Cook, and Max Cavanaugh.

The auditors furnished men for a continuous audit, which kept the financial affairs of the Fund under constant scrutiny.

That, together with two expert public accountants brought in to act as budget comptrollers—Rowe Steel and Walter Riepert—constituted the balance of the national staff organization. And naturally, it didn't all happen overnight.

The fact is that it took just about eight weeks to progress from the original meeting on December 15, 1942, to the formal opening of a staffed and equipped office on February 8, 1943; an office originally established in the Empire State Building, but soon to be moved to larger quarters at 46 Cedar Street, in downtown New York.

FINANCING THE FUND

Meantime, while the staff was busy with plans and schedules, the Fund's Treasurer, Gordon S. Rentschler, had a bit of financing to do, a general description of which is worth recording as a pattern for future use.

In light of the fact that campaigns for the Fund were not to be held until the following Fall—ten months away—and that payments to the Fund could not be expected in any volume until a month or two later than that, there were two problems to consider; the immediate financing of the Fund's administrative expenses, and the financing of the agencies beginning June 1, 1943—the date on which agency agreements were to become effective.

The immediate requirements for both purposes were met by a series of loans by the National City Bank, beginning in February, and by June reaching a peak of $3,835,000.

Arrangements were then made through the National City Bank to syndicate a loan for $17,500,000 with a group of 76 banks, representing all sections of the country; with interest at one and a half per cent, and with the understanding that funds could be drawn as needed, beginning July 1, 1943, and that the loan was to be paid off on or before January 31, 1944.

Under this arrangement, $8,750,000 was borrowed on July 13th, with the other half of the loan taken up as funds were needed, in August, September, and October. By December, funds from the first appeal had flowed in to retire all but $5,250,000 of the obligation. On January 10, 1944, the loan was paid in full.

Similar arrangements were set up for the second year, but it was not found necessary to borrow funds until early in October, and then for $7,000,000 only; a loan then retired in four equal instalments, ending on December 4, 1944. No further bank financing was required from that time on.

There are five noteworthy points about this financing:

First, this was a "character loan," in that the only initial security behind it was confidence and goodwill. Such an arrangement could hardly be made without strong and reputable national leadership.

Second, the opportunity to participate in the loan was deliberately extended to a large number of banks, in all sections of the country, instead of merely to a few of the great banks in only a few major cities. This had the advantage, to be sure, of spreading whatever risk was entailed, but the principal reason lay in the field of public relations. For to acquaint the boards of directors of 76 banks with the full story of the National War Fund, several months in advance of the public appeal, was one of the easiest ways to make sure that responsible business leaders in all parts of the United States knew what the Fund was, knew the importance of its task, and had confidence in its success; with the result that they were ready to champion its cause in their own local communities.

Third, while the loan was in force and before the Treasurer started to pay it off, we saw to it that each of the participating banks was sent an occasional progress report. This was probably good public relations procedure, and was unquestionably good publicity for the Fund.

Fourth, the way the loan was repaid demonstrated a fact well-known to bankers but perhaps not so obvious to others: namely, that one of the ways to establish good credit is not to need it. After the original loan was repaid before the date it was due, no persuasion was necessary in establishing a loaning syndicate for the second year.

Finally, it was found that the very existence of such a loan was a powerful lever on advance solicitation and on collections from local chests. One of the most telling points in asking for advance gifts from national corporations, and in asking the major local chests to hasten their remittances, both in 1943 and 1944, was that early cash would save interest. This did save interest, and was one of the major reasons why it was found possible to borrow only $7,000,000 in the second year.

OTHER NATIONAL MOVES

With the Fund organized nationally in terms of corporate structure and committee personnel, staff, headquarters, and preliminary financing, there were three other major essentials from the national point of view which had to be completed before the full procedure of organization could be extended to the states.

Most obvious was an early pattern for state organization. We had an advantage here in that several states, as will be seen later, had already been organized on their own initiative. First of all, then, we obtained these patterns and simply passed them around. Meanwhile, however, based on the current patterns and previous experience, the national staff turned out as rapidly as possible a 12-page booklet, "Suggested Procedure for State Campaign Organization." (See Appendix D.)

Almost as obvious was the early need for a state quota system, so that each state could be told its fair percentage of any national goal. How this was done will be related elsewhere; the point to be made here is that such a quota system is an essential preliminary to state organization.

Not at all obvious, it was found, was the equal necessity for establishing the amount of the national budget as soon as possible, as another essential for state organization; the reason being, as experience had proved, that prospective state leaders always wanted to know not only their proportionate share, as a percentage, but also what this meant in their particular state in terms of dollars. And this was not mere idle curiosity. They had to know the state figure in order to persuade others to serve, and in order to have a solid base for discussing the project with leaders in local communities. It was all part of the package they were being asked to sell.

The reason the need for an early budget was not at all obvious was that it was theoretically illogical and locally without precedent.

The counterargument was made, for example, that no national budget could fairly be established until the budget committee had heard all the agency budgets. Those whose experience had been chiefly with local chests also pointed out, equally reasonably, that campaign goals in local communities were never established prior to campaign organization; that on the contrary, the decision on goal was always deferred as long as possible, to enable the local chest to adjust its objective as closely as possible to conditions current at campaign time. (Harry Wareham, it is recalled, argued that the chest campaigns in Rochester, opening traditionally on Monday, never settled the goal question until the immediately previous Friday.)

Those of us, however, who had participated in the 1941 and 1942 financing of the USO felt that the problem of the National War Fund was a wholly different one; not merely because it was a new and unknown enterprise, as the chest in Rochester was not, but chiefly because of the inexorable time requirements of a national schedule. If appeals were to be made everywhere in October—not only in organized chest cities, but literally everywhere—local committees had to be ready in September, county organizations ready in August, county chairmen enlisted by July, district chairmen in June, and state organizations completed in May. This all added up to the fact that state chairmen had to be sought out and enlisted for service not later than May first, and preferably sooner. And accepting the premise that state chairmen won't start until they know the amount they are being asked to raise—a premise experience had demonstrated to be true—the conclusion was that we had to know the national objective, whether or not such an early determination was either logical or without local precedent.

The goal, therefore, was set at $125,000,000 on May 3, 1943. Agency budgets were established at a later date, and simply had to be accommodated within that total. And that is the way it has to be done on any national fund-raising campaign whenever the cause is new, and whenever the amount the participating agencies could effectively spend is obviously more than the amount that can be raised. You take a look at the record, you take into account what the national figure would mean in terms of local goals in a number of representative communities, you ask a lot of people about it in order to get the maximum participation in the final decision, and then you do something for which the Interstate Commerce Commission has spanked railroads ever since 1887; you ask for all you think the traffic will bear.

All of these moves, as one can readily imagine, took quite a bit of doing, but they were all out of the way by the time the goal question was settled. Then we were ready to start back to the grass roots, by carrying the organization process to the state and local levels.

STATE ORGANIZATION

And now we come to the part that is just a bit fabulous; how the state war funds were organized.

As previously explained, we did have a pattern, in our "Suggested Procedure for State Campaign Organization." But the difficulty, from the point of view of anyone seeking a simple chronicle of how the task was done, is that no two states followed precisely the same method. The pattern was sound, and is still to be recommended. But patterns have a way of getting mixed up with people.

For the full details, students would have to seek out the individual state histories, most of which, by now, have been deposited with state librarians or with the librarians of state universities.

The gist of the story, however, can be told by reciting some four general patterns; with one of which every state can be identified in all but a few minor details.

First, four states had already organized state-wide war chests before the National War Fund itself was organized. Alabama and Rhode Island had run successful state campaigns in 1942. Arizona and Indiana were organized too late for 1942 campaigns, but were ready to go by the time the National War Fund was ready to function. In all four states, the initiative was taken by lay leaders and executives of local community chests.

Second, after the formation of the National War Fund was announced in January, 1943, eight states were organized by spontaneous combustion, entirely on their own initiative: California, Connecticut, Illinois, Massachusetts, Michigan, New Hampshire, Ohio, and Pennsylvania. In New Hampshire, the initiative was taken by interested businessmen. In the other seven states, community chest executives took the lead, usually by following one of the state patterns already established elsewhere.

That left only 36 states to be organized on the initiative of the National War Fund. These fell into two groups, constituting the third and fourth of the general patterns.

Third, then, were 12 states organized by national initiative on a transfer device. In these states, the USO state campaign organization of 1942 became the state war funds of 1943; usually with the same state leadership and staff. Included were Georgia, Kentucky, New Jersey, New Mexico, South Carolina, South Dakota, Tennessee, Utah, Vermont, West Virginia, Wisconsin, and Wyoming.

Finally, in the fourth general pattern fell the other 24 states, in which national initiative was called upon to help set up state war funds as wholly new instrumentalities. It is in this category that the procedure followed has some historical significance, as a pattern others can follow.

The procedure began at national headquarters, by assembling for each of the states the fullest possible list of state leaders who had previously been active on behalf of one or more of the individual agencies. Every state had had a USO chairman in 1942, and many had had chairmen for United China Relief. In addition, many agencies which had not been organized on state lines were able to supply the names of local chairmen—particularly for the larger cities. Properly classified, and with appropriate comment from the agencies, these names were the initial ammunition with which fieldworkers set out to help organize state war funds.

A word here is in order on how this organizing task was divided. Partly on ease of access, determined by the routes of railroads and airlines, and partly by the relative state quotas involved, the country was divided into three regions: roughly the Coast and Western states, the states in the valley of the Mississippi (including the Southeast), and the states east of Indiana and north of North Carolina.

For each of these regions there was an Assistant Campaign Director at national headquarters, and a travelling representative in the field. At the outset, however, nearly everyone took to the field in order to get things moving as fast as possible in the maximum number of concurrent state actions.

Armed, then, with a list of potential leaders, and with all the available literature, the fieldman's next move was to initiate a series of rapid-fire consultations within a state, looking toward an agreement by some informal group on who was the right man to lead the state effort.

Then came the process of invitation; preferably by the informal but indigenous group in the state, seconded by a formal approach from national headquarters, by wire or telephone. In many instances, the Governor of the state was helpful in persuading the state chairman to agree to serve.

With a chairman signed up, the next move was to engage a state director and find state headquarters; tasks on which national headquarters stood ready to help, by suggesting personnel and if necessary by advancing funds for initial expenses.

From there on, the same pattern was followed all over again, within the state itself. In turn, to a less degree, the procedure was followed later in the respective counties.

Campaign organizations were also set up, it should be added, in Alaska, Hawaii (through affiliation with the Honolulu chest), the Panama Canal Zone, the Virgin Islands, and later in Puerto Rico. Field trips were found necessary in Puerto Rico and the Virgin Islands, but elsewhere the organization was initiated by wire and by mail. Without initiation, substantial collections were made among members of American colonies in 13 other countries. These groups, like many states, simply organized themselves.

If there is any one point about the organization process that should be stressed above all others, it is undoubtedly the point that everything depends on the quality of the leadership. Nothing that was learned about organization in all three years of the National War Fund could approach in importance the fact that active and devoted leadership, both lay and professional, was the one sure key to success.

Nothing was more dangerous, we used to say, than the second-class attention of a first-class man; far better it was, we learned, to have the first-class attention of a second-class man. Stuffed shirts may look mighty fine in a laundry, but in a campaign they look too much like a shroud.

That one fundamental is of such transcendental importance that one is tempted to say, as Hillel said, that that is the Law; all the rest is merely commentary.

But there are, in fact, a few more observations to be made in order to fill in the corners of the picture.

The first is that the originating group in any fund-raising enterprise should be representative of the groups from which funds are to be sought. King George III had some difficulty in understanding that simple principle; and sad to say, the same difficulty persists to this day in certain states and local communities. So because the National War Fund wished to appeal to everyone, and not merely to the carriage trade, we strongly and constantly urged that state and local committees should include in their memberships representatives from as many groups as possible: nationality groups, organized labor, businessmen, farmers, patriotic societies, and so on, to a true cross-section of American life.

The second is that a healthy organization must be nourished by accurate and interesting information. There may be places in this world where the people will work valiantly for causes they know little or nothing about, but you can put it down as so much very fine gospel that it couldn't happen here.

The third has to do with a paradox of American human nature. One of the most gregarious people in the world, we like to say, and frequently do, that we hate to go to meetings. And there was justification for that point of view under war-time travel conditions. The result was, and probably always will be, a cry for doing it by mail, by bulletins and memoranda, by wire and by telephone.

All these devices we used, and many more. But you can also put down as gospel the fact that in organization, as in any other adjustment of human relations, there is no satisfactory substitute for face-to-face personal contact. And that means meetings; national conferences at least twice a year, state meetings at least at quarterly intervals, local meetings as often as once a week.

These, at any rate, were the ways and the doctrines by which the National War Fund, itself the result of a grass-roots demand, built the channels of organization by which a grass-roots response could send widely collected dollars on widely scattered errands of goodwill.

The one thing that made it possible to organize so swiftly and so well was that the Fund was essentially a mandate; what it sought to do was what nearly everyone wanted. It was that most powerful of causes—an idea born of the people, and born at the right time.

IV

LETTING THE LIGHT
SO SHINE

For the eyes of the trade alone, the technical story of the National War Fund's publicity program would be a statistical delight; seldom has so much been seen and heard by so many people, so many times, at so little cost.

In these pages, however, remembering our purpose of leaving a trail others can follow, we shall seek to confine the chronicle to a few of the main signposts—aims, problems, procedure, material, media, organization, costs, and general findings.

AIMS

One of the great common-sense truths of human endeavor is that the first step in any procedure should be to define the task; to make sure that you know precisely what you are going to try to do. (And lest that should appear to be just so much superfluous sententiousness, let it be stated here that many an affair has come a cropper because its aims were confused.)

First of all, then, it should be recorded that the National War Fund sought to use the rifle instead of the shotgun; aiming at the bull's-eye of certain specific targets, rather than sending shots broadcast in the hope of chance hits.

Because ours was a temporary enterprise related solely to the period of the war, we had no reason to indulge in institutional aims, such as trying to win public approval and long-term acceptance for the National War Fund in itself. And because we wanted every possible penny of each dollar to go to the purposes the Fund sought to serve, economy dictated that we simplify our purposes and waste no ammunition.

From the beginning, therefore, the Fund's public program addressed itself primarily to the simple task of helping local campaigns to be successful. While we cooperated with the agencies in interpreting

35

their programs, our major task was backing up the fund-raising process in local communities, by helping to identify these local campaigns with the total task of winning the war, and by preaching constantly the doctrine of universality, that "Everyone wants to give, and nearly everyone does."

This simplicity of aim is believed to have been sound in its original conception, and certainly proved sound in practice.

PROBLEMS

Any national effort, such as the National War Fund, tomorrow or any time, faces six big problems in the area of publicity.

The first is one of timing; the same problem faced by Sears and Roebuck every time they produce their famous catalog. So much can happen while the train is in the long, dark tunnel of design, writing, printing, and distribution.

Under war-time conditions, the tunnel was longer than ever. In fact, the poster to appear on October billboards had to go into production not later than March, which meant that the artist had to finish in February a design discussed one or two months before. At least ten months ahead, therefore, it was necessary to guess what the war situation would be, and what central theme, accordingly, should be stressed at fund-raising time.

The second problem is the complex problem of identification. What are you going to call your enterprise, so that it will mean substantially the same thing in every community?

Now if you are entirely on your own everywhere, as in the case of the American Red Cross, the problem is simple; it's the American Red Cross campaign in every city, town, and village of the United States. But the problem is far from simple if your cause is to be federated with other causes, in local community chests.

This is one place where the National War Fund innocently stubbed its newborn toe. Its name turned out to be a poorly selected one, for two reasons.

For one thing, it proved to be confusing, when the U. S. Treasury and the American Red Cross were found later to be referring to the funds they sought to raise as "national war funds." The name was too generic.

The other reason was that the word "national," in any federated appeal, had meaning on the national level only. On the state level, experience proved, the tendency was to use the term, "Ohio War

Fund" and not the "National War Fund of Ohio." Locally, the terminology problem was even worse. Community chests changed their names, to include the war-related appeals, but by no standard pattern. Some were war funds, some war chests, and all sought, naturally enough, to make clear the local identification.

The result, unhappily, was that radio network programs about the "National War Fund" were likely to fall on virtually deaf ears in St. Louis, where everyone was asked to give to the Greater St. Louis War Chest, and were therefore apt to think that the "National War Fund" was some different cause.

"United War Fund," by the wisdom of hindsight, would have been the right name; meaningful nationally, to each state, and in every community.

Think well, then, before you name that future cause.

The third problem is production. Even in the brave new world this is likely to make for migraine; in finding printers who can do the work in the desired volume and on time, in locating the essential quantity of paper, in finding envelopes, in getting enough cartons for the shipping process, et cetera *ad nauseam*. To record much of what happened during the war in this area would awaken too many painful memories, among too many good production men who even now are still feebly licking their wounds. Let us, then, decently draw the veil by merely warning Posterity that it takes longer than you think to turn out printed materials for a national appeal—much, much longer. Start early, trust nobody, and believe the delivery only when you see it.

Akin to production, but a man-sized problem in its own right, is the problem of distribution. Here too can be found a fine assortment of headaches, the chief remedies for which are to keep a good control system at national headquarters, but to decentralize deliveries. The way madness lies is to say "F. O. B. National Headquarters." Establish shipping points at state offices, or regional points, or anywhere under the heading of "elsewhere"; then let the vendors ship direct to those places, on written instructions. At the National War Fund, it took two men and several girls to keep such distribution machinery going, even under maximum decentralization; and they were very good people indeed.

The fifth problem, by natural sequence, is the problem of visibility. And the reason this is a major problem is that the finest publicity material in the world can easily end up on a shelf or in a wastebasket. That is why the problem of visibility is something to be considered at the outset, and not after the material has been produced. There is no use in having posters unless you first make sure that boards will be available for them, at the time you want them shown; and the same thing holds true for radio platters, magazine articles, stories for newspapers, and so on.

Finally, as problem number six, is that of economy. Everybody must know that it costs money to raise money, but nobody, perhaps most of all those who have to spend it on a charitable cause, wants to spend any more than is really necessary. The problem, therefore, is not in spending too much; the nub of the difficulty, usually, is in making sure that you spend enough. At any rate, budgeting the publicity program, necessarily done in advance, is a major problem that should be noted here, as part of the essential background for this publicity review.

PROCEDURE

"All right," says the sturdy reader who has read this far, "I see what your aims and problems were. But what did you do? How did you go about it?"

First of all, someone has to hit the good ship with a bottle of champagne. You have to name it, and you have to launch it. And the way we did it was effective enough, but hardly original; we used the White House soundingboard.

Early in January, after a Washington dateline, "President Roosevelt announced today, at a White House press conference, the organization of a National War Fund, which next October will make a joint appeal in every county in the United States on behalf of . . ."

Soon thereafter, to all local chests, to the local constituencies of the member agencies, to the press, and to everywhere else we thought it would help, we sent a four-page leaflet, "A Federation of War Philanthropies," describing the purpose of the Fund, listing the causes to be served, the amounts tentatively allocated to each, and the names of the Fund's officers and directors. These were the two preliminary announcements; the flourish of trumpets leading to the major task of striking up the band.

For a time, the development of public acceptance for the Fund had to be left to the missionary work of field organizers, to discussion at the national and regional meetings of community chests, and to whatever publicity opportunities chance afforded. For there was much work to be done.

That work began with the appointment of several working volunteer committees, and with the organization of the necessary headquarters staff.

Other procedural points worth recording have to do with the record, the process of orientation, and the method for review and approval. All three involve useful precedents.

From the beginning, the publicity department, like all other departments of the Fund, kept careful records; all the way from a daily report on the activities of every member of the staff up to an annual report on the work for that particular year. This involved some degree of tedious self-discipline, but the result is that anyone who cares to check the detail can find what happened, who did it, when it was done, what it cost, and most of the time some current comment on the effectiveness or lack of effectiveness of this or that. It kept everyone posted without wasting time in conferences, and made a record by which each year's special planning could be checked against detailed experience.

Another sound procedure was to take periodic sights along the way in order to keep well oriented with the two main groups that fundamentally were the bosses of the publicity program—the agencies of the Fund, and the people who had to raise the money. Every now and then, therefore, the publicity staff would meet with the representatives of the agencies, and then confer with state and local war fund executives. Unanimity, of course, was beyond expectation, but it tended to keep the air clear, and just possibly may have won friends and influenced people.

The process of review and approval was kept simple and centralized. Things had to move swiftly, and past experience had taught us all that not the least of the blemishes on this always imperfect world is the sad fact that no two people—least of all two authorities—can agree on the merits of the simplest sample of pure reading matter. So we let the advertising experts agree on the advertising, but on printed material, newspaper copy, and radio scripts we did the approving ourselves, going to Higher Authority only on matters which in the staff's own opinion involved questions of basic policy.

We have implied that this saved time, and saved money on "author's corrections" in printing bills. We'll go further, by asserting that it also saved a lot of material from the mediocrity of multiple compromise.

MATERIAL

No mere catalog of all the publicity materials of the National War Fund would be of much interest in an account of this kind.

On the other hand, it is at least conceivable that there might be some general interest in what types of publicity material are required in any national promotion, and how they are shaped for local use.

It will help you to follow this if you remember that publicity material falls cosily into a series of opposite compartments: technical and public, national and local, and immediate and deferred.

The technical material, advising other people how to do things you can't always do yourself, includes a manual and chart talk for speakers, an advertising kit, a photograph catalog, a facts folder for editors and writers, a kit for local radio programs, a clipsheet of ready-made newspaper material, and a general "casebook," or guide for local publicity directors, covering everything from the handling of news to the arrangement of local window displays. Other items may be added as desired, but these are the basic necessities.

The public material, almost needless to say, includes the material for all the potential contributors. And this in turn falls into two classifications; general messages for everybody, and material designed for individual consumption.

In the general category are radio programs, advertising, magazine articles, posters, window cards and displays, car cards, motion pictures, newspaper articles, cartoons and photographs, speeches, and stickers for restaurant menus. All of these were in the program of the National War Fund, and by experience were found useful or necessary.

The real pay-off, however, was in the material designed for individual use—the material placed in the hands of a volunteer solicitor, to be given personally to a potential contributor. This was the real stuff to give the troops.

If you want to discard everything else and get down to the barest publicity essentials for raising money in a broad public appeal, all you really need is a small leaflet (we called it "the mass distribution piece"), a subscription blank, and some device by which the giver can demonstrate that he has given—almost always a button or pin, and in our case the addition of a small sticker for a house window or the rear window of an automobile. Thousands of local campaigns in smaller cities and towns were run with nothing else.

Again, the material is either national or local. And for maximum visibility the National War Fund used national material as sparingly as possible, only when circumstances made it obviously impossible to localize it. It had to be national in magazines, on radio networks, in Pullman cars, and on such occasions as a White House press conference. But nearly everything else was localized. And that was what made for maximum visibility.

Our leaflets left a space for imprinting locally the name of the community campaign. Almost all the material for newspapers was designed for release by the local chairman—"So and so is the situation, according to word received here by Joseph Q. Doakes, chairman of the United War Fund of Springfield..." And even on the posters for the big billboards we always called attention to the space for pasting on an extra strip of paper to identify the cause locally. That, and similar devices, constitutes the localization of publicity material prepared nationally. And all the returns show it pays to do it that way.

The final dual classification, immediate and deferred, embraces the distinction newspapermen make between "spot news" and "time copy." Candidly, we throw this in merely to complete the series, for the fact is that you can't handle "spot news"—reports of events as they actually occur on a given day—and at the same time localize its release. Even for the press associations, we specialized on the "time copy," which within reasonable limits could be used any time there was space for it.

Finally, on the subject of material, it should be pointed out that while our message was meant for everyone, we did have to take into account the need for certain special literature for special groups. As any such national effort would have to do, we prepared a special pamphlet "for officers and directors of American corporations," sponsored other special material for members of trade-unions, and sent specially prepared news data to the Negro press. But all these were just so many candles on the cake, and have little to do with the cake's basic recipe.

MEDIA

For a quick look at the channels through which publicity was made to flow, we might take a quick run through the media:

Advertising. The volunteer advertising committee, organized through the War Advertising Council, prepared in a typical year 18,000 portfolios containing proof sheets of some 70 advertisements for either national or local use, ranging in size from a few full-page newspaper advertisements to single-column advertisements measuring a few inches only. These were distributed primarily through the state war funds, with requests for the desired mats, electrotypes, or stereotypes to be sent to the nearest of four distribution centers of the

Western Newspaper Union. Agencies and national advertisers were also supplied with a special 16-page pamphlet on ways in which to publicize the Fund, distributed by and under the imprint of the War Advertising Council.

Billboard and window posters produced and exhibited through the Advertising Committee were given space in each of the three campaigns with a commercial value of more than two million dollars.

Radio. This program was in three parts: (1) furnishing a fact sheet about the Fund and its agencies for the radio stations and advertising agencies which produced the network programs allocated by the Office of War Information; (2) preparing a radio kit to help in the preparation of local programs and (3) the production of some 4,000 electrical transcriptions for the ready use of any one broadcasting station. In the final year, from September 17 to October 15, the material reached 590 network and national spot programs, with 850,780,000 estimated "listener impressions." Anyone who listened to the radio at all, during the Fund's radio season, was bound to hear the story.

Magazines. Here too the volunteer committee prepared a special kit, for the editors and publishers of national magazines, and also obtained statements or articles from a long list of nationally prominent authors. As a result of these two moves, and some 200 personal calls at editorial offices, a typical year found magazine mention of the Fund in more than 500 magazines and trade papers, through cover designs, editorials, pictures, cartoons, articles, and so on.

Motion Pictures. Through the cooperation of the Office of War Information and the War Activities Committee of the Motion Picture Industry, there was produced each year a ten-minute motion picture, shown in 13,000 motion-picture houses. The Fund, in turn, used some 2,200 copies in the smaller 16-millimeter size for state and local campaign meetings, and some 1,800 copies of a 35-millimeter trailer— a special two-minute picture to be used in local theatres at campaign time—with room for 25 words of a local announcement.

Speakers Bureau. This phase of any national publicity effort could well be termed the neuropsychiatric division, or the Burns and Bruises Bureau. Every local campaign, it would seem, feels justified sooner or later in calling upon national headquarters to produce for the opening meeting a trio comprising General Eisenhower, Admiral Nimitz, and Bob Hope. In this connection, there are two nuggets of wisdom to be tucked away for posterity: first, "name" speakers are less useful and reliable than the relative unknowns who know the story from beginning to end, and who have seen personally what they have to talk about; and second, speaking dates should be arranged in the sequence of planned tours, with the state organizations doing the local booking. The most effective and dependable speakers, in the experience of the National War Fund, were agency representatives who had recently returned from abroad, representatives of countries served by the member agencies, and performers who had recently returned from overseas duty with USO-Camp Shows. During the height of each campaign, some 60 such speakers were on the road, each making an average of five speeches a day.

Other Media. Material was sent regularly, of course, to local committees, for the use of local newspapers, and to press associations and national syndicates. Special promotions included posters in all the Pullman cars, special advertisements in mail-order catalogs, postmark designs for automatic mailing machines, bulletins for the program committees of women's clubs and conventions, special articles for house organs, trade papers and trade magazines, and a special issue of "True Comics" under the sponsorship of the Parents Institute.

ORGANIZATION

The over-all direction of publicity for the Fund was in the hands of a volunteer Committee on Public Relations, headed in the first year by Henry M. Wriston, with Thomas D'Arcy Brophy as chairman of the advertising committee. Mr. Brophy headed the entire volunteer organization in the last two years.

As shown in some detail in the appendix, the volunteer organization comprised a publication advertising committee, a radio committee, an outdoor and poster advertising committee, a magazine committee, and a motion-picture committee.

The staff, under the direction of David M. Church, varied with the seasonal load, and at the annual peak averaged eleven persons—as industrious and devoted a crew as one could hope to find.

COSTS

If the publicity program of the Fund had been duplicated commercially, the total cost, by the estimates of the War Advertising Council, would have reached at least $30,000,000.

Because so much talent, time, and space were contributed, however, the net cost for the three years was less than a million dollars—despite the somewhat astronomical quantities in which certain supplies had to be distributed.

In 1945, for example, the Fund produced 32,580,000 tags for contributors, at a cost of 44 cents per thousand, and 32,000,000 window stickers, at a cost of 93 cents per thousand. Unit costs were reasonable enough, but the quantities needed necessarily involved many thousands of dollars of expense.

GENERAL FINDINGS

If one had to select pieces of general advice for the future, on points to watch in a national publicity promotion for some common federated cause, the points we would stress would be these:

1. Consider the name of the enterprise, and its accompanying symbolism, in the light of its local identification.

2. Build your committee around a group of volunteer workers, rather than a jury of consulting experts. The committee should be down on the field with the team, and not merely up in the cheering section.

3. Define clearly at the outset the specific aims and functions to be covered successively at each level—national, state, and local.

4. With all due regard for local autonomy and the desirability of giving local committees what they ask for, confine the menu of publicity materials to the minimum number of items—the lowest common denominator of items definitely required by the average local campaign. This will result in some squawks, but in material economies. Moreover, you will raise just as much money.

5. As far as possible, see that everything is decentralized, for the reason that maximum visibility and maximum economy depend on what is done locally.

6. Remember that time is always of the essence; invariably, in a national program, "it's later than you think."

V

HARVEST TIME

The aim of this chapter is not merely to record how money was raised for the agencies of the National War Fund, but to present a workable pattern for raising money for any cause with a universal appeal, national or local.

That double aim necessitates our first considering a few simple fundamentals: (1) what is meant by an effective fund-raising campaign; (2) the five essential elements for such a campaign; (3) ten laws or principles which through the years have been found to govern campaign results; and (4) certain standards or yardsticks which most campaigns should seek to attain or observe.

After that, it will be in order to deal historically with the experience of the National War Fund in methods and results—an experience believed to be no different, as far as the application of those fundamentals is concerned, than raising money to build a new church or hospital.

DEFINITION

First, then, let us see what we mean when we say "fund-raising campaign." For while we Americans use those words more often than any other people in the world, there is still far too little enlightenment or agreement on what the words involve. Here, for instance, are five common misconceptions about effective fund-raising:

1. *The William Jennings Bryan Complex.* Before World War I, you oldsters may remember, Mr. Bryan thundered his rebuttal to the preparedness warnings of the great Teddy Roosevelt by the confident assertion that "a million men would spring to arms overnight." People who wish to raise money sometimes make the same costly mistake, by assuming happily that if the cause is well publicized, and the people are told where to leave their gifts, the money will roll in.

2. *The Mike and Ike Delusion.* Rube Goldberg's "Mike and Ike— They Look Alike" was a great cartoon idea, as Lewis Carroll could

45

have easily prophesied. But the concept is just so much virulent poison to effective fund-raising, whenever people begin to have the bright idea that everyone should give a dime or a dollar, or that a hundred should give a thousand, or come up with any of those apparently easy schemes that raise money merely by long division and the multiplication table. To be sure, you can raise some money that way, but usually at shockingly high cost.

3. *The Saturday Night Shave.* You'll know what we mean by this if your shave of Saturday morning doesn't look so good when you get ready to go out in the evening; you just give it "the once-over lightly." That's all right with a beard, but it is almost always fatal in a fund-raising campaign, for the basic reason that success never comes the easy way, and always requires careful planning and preparation and a lot of hard work.

4. *The Cinderella Dream.* You can call this the Cult of the Ostrich, and it will mean the same thing—a blind hope that everything will come out all right. People responsible for fund-raising campaigns are fooled too often because the first response comes easily, and because realism and objectivity are lost in the clouds of starry-eyed wishful thinking.

5. *The Pattern of the Losing Football Coach.* When you can't win, it may be comforting to reflect that you are building character. But those who want nothing less than victory in a fund-raising campaign should always take heed, if not actually do a little viewing with alarm, when the campaign managers start talking about "the larger, long-term gains in making new friends for the institution." To be sure, a fund-raising campaign is a public relations operation from start to finish; the design, however, should be for giving.

The trouble with these and similar misconceptions about fund-raising, all of them cobwebs we must first strike aside if we are to see clearly what a campaign really is, is that they fail to take into account the five essentials for successful fund-raising, and certain of the laws or principles which no campaign can ever escape.

Cobwebs aside, then, we can define a fund-raising campaign affirmatively as "a planned mobilization of the friends of a cause or institution, for a voluntary solicitation of proportionate gifts from an informed constituency; always toward a specific goal or objective, and usually within a specified period of time." Neither Webster nor Churchill might approve of that phraseology, but we think it covers the ground.

FIVE ESSENTIAL ELEMENTS

Under that or an equivalent definition, an organized fund-raising campaign comprises five basic elements. You need the four to make the watch, and you need the fifth to make it tick:

First, in chronological order rather than in order of importance, a good campaign needs a strong and timely case; an aim plainly in the interest of those who will be asked to give—rather than merely in the interest of an agency or institution *per se*—and a program reasonable enough to let the mind rationalize what the heart prompts the giver to do.

Most important of all, but placed second because you usually have to have a good case to get it, is active and influential leadership. Without such leadership many a good cause has withered on the vine; with it, you can accomplish almost anything. You need it at the top, in terms of the first-class attention of a first-class man, and you need it all the way through the campaign organization, at each successive level—leadership that is active and influential, by getting out in front and leading, in a way others will be willing and ready to follow.

Third, a successful campaign needs a sufficient number of informed and enthusiastic volunteer workers—the sales force to sell the cause. The right kind of a volunteer worker is someone with some good reasons for giving liberally and proportionately to some good cause, and who is enthusiastically determined, at some particular time, to see someone and ask for some money. Persons who fail to qualify are those who "just can't say 'no' to the team captain," those who are really terribly busy but might be willing to "take a few names," and particularly those who do nothing more but write a few begging letters. How many volunteer workers are needed, of course, depends on how many people are to be solicited, with variations in the usual proportion of one worker to every ten prospective contributors, depending on the ease or difficulty of personal access and how big a load the workers are ready to carry. (The ladies, God bless 'em, will usually take more names to see than the men will.)

The fourth essential is a campaign constituency, or field of support, in which the known giving potential is commensurate with the campaign goal. A good list of such potential contributors is one in which every name has been carefully selected, all pertinent data accurately transcribed, each card rated by competent volunteers for its individual quota or amount to be sought, and all cards finally classified for easy assignment. All of which requires (1) a good reason for the inclusion of each card, (2) painstaking research, (3) meticulous typing and clerical work, (4) volunteer rating committees, and (5) some simple and economical system of card control.

The fifth essential, for lack of a better term, we'll call campaign dynamics. If you've made a good watch by qualifying your campaign on the first four essentials, this is what you need to make the watch tick—the catalytic agent to put the mixture to the boil. In its essence, campaign dynamics involves the routines of planning, timing, direction, and operation. But you could just as well say that it involves the skillful manipulation of the laws of human behavior by competent campaign management.

And now, assuming agreement on what fund-raising really is, and what its basic essentials are, let us look at the main body of the law—the rules or principles which have been found to affect all such voluntary campaign efforts.

PRINCIPLES OF FUND-RAISING

One of the pleasanter aspects of the profession of one who makes fund-raising his vocation is that the wiser such a man gets, the more he shrinks from being called an expert. He comes to feel, after a time, that the more he learns the less he really knows. Which, after all, is as it should be. For fund-raising, such an old-timer would tell you, is more of an art than a science, and an art in a relatively primitive stage.

Nevertheless, when you see such and such an effect invariably follow such and such a cause, over a long period of time, you come to share the privilege of the Messrs. Boyle and Charles—you can say you have observed a law, which your colleagues or contemporaries are at liberty to challenge if they can.

Here, then, are ten such laws of raising money, with which the fund-raising fraternity are believed to be in virtually unanimous agreement:

1. The quantitative result of every fund-raising campaign varies directly with the quality and devotion of the leadership.

2. The effectiveness of any campaign organization can be measured by the extent to which responsibility is decentralized, by the planned distribution of assimilable work units.

3. Personal contact, whether for the enlistment of workers or the solicitation of gifts, should be established on the same or higher level.

4. Duly proportionate quotas or goals, whether for dollars or units of work, should be established and accepted for every part of the total

campaign structure: for every division, every team, every worker, and every prospective contributor.

5. In any multiple fund-raising effort, where there is likelihood that some units will succeed and some will fail, total success can be assured only by adopting in advance either one or both of two measures: including in the goal an extra amount as a cushion or safety factor against unit failures, or an agreement that successful units will either pay the full amounts raised, regardless of quotas, or will share such oversubscriptions in some equable proportion.

6. Campaigns are best conducted in an atmosphere of universality—a general public impression that everyone will benefit and that nearly everyone will wish to participate in a certain way, and at a certain time.

7. The effectiveness of campaign organization is limited by the law of diminishing returns: the wider its periphery, the lower the returns and the greater the proportionate cost.

8. To paraphrase Shakespeare, if a campaign were to be done, 'twere well it were done quickly; in communities, as in kindergartens, attention periods have their limits.

9. You can't raise money without spending money; within reasonable limits the return is likely to be commensurate with the investment.

10. Every good campaign is essentially a public relations operation—an aggregate of the tremendous trifles by which any enterprise wins and holds public approval: good manners, pleasurable experiences, recognition for achievement, and proof that all the sacrifice anyone made was worth far more than its cost.

STANDARDS

Finally, before taking up the story of the actual methods by which money was raised for the National War Fund, let us wander in the area of norms and standards, both because it may be helpful to other causes, and because it may throw more light on the Fund's own procedures. Primarily, this involves standards for timing and quotas. Incidentally, it should cover standards for so-called "benefits," and for fund-raising costs.

Timing. Nothing could be more important than standards for timing, for if the timing is wrong, everything is wrong. Certain steps have to be taken in a certain order, and if they are not taken at the right time—well, you can just run that campaign later on, perhaps next year.

Nationally, in an appeal such as that of the National War Fund or the American Red Cross, preparations have to start nearly a year ahead—not less than ten months. It might be helpful here to cite this general timetable for any national cause which hopes to associate itself with local chest campaigns in October and November.

December—settle general theme or dominant idea around which artists can start work on poster designs, and copy writers can produce a preliminary printed statement as a basis for enlisting national and state leadership.

January—complete staffing of national headquarters, draft general plan for national and state procedure, and if possible establish national goal, for advance review by National Budget Committee.

February—preliminary cultivation of leaders and executives of local community chests at the national meeting of Community Chests and Councils, Inc.—usually held in the Midwest, and ordinarily attended by representatives from all the big cities except New York City, and from hundreds of medium-sized cities and towns from coast to coast.

March—complete state quota system, and suggested intrastate quotas for every county. (Posters and printed matter should be in production by this time, much of it for delivery in June.)

April—May—complete national and state organizations.

June—July—states are now organizing the counties, and are negotiating for inclusion by local community chests at regular meetings of local budget committees.

August—September—Counties are organizing towns and rural areas. If there is to be any solicitation on the national level, this is when it should be done, so that the results can be used as giving examples in the local campaigns opening in October.

(All this time, incidentally, if yours is a repeating campaign, you are working hard to collect the money that was raised for your cause in the previous year.)

On the state level, things should start happening in the late spring. Generalizations can easily be carried too far, in light of the fact that there are only three counties in Delaware and 254 in Texas, but an average state would proceed about like this:

May—chairman and state executive appointed. Headquarters staffed and equipped. Work starts on breaking down state quota into county quotas, taking into account the state expense and a factor of safety.

June—state meeting, principally for indoctrination, and approval of county quotas. State representatives start negotiating for inclusion by community chests.

July—regional meetings, for representatives from counties in natural geographical groupings, principally for enlistment of county chairmen. State should know by this time whether cause is to be included by community chests.

August—county meetings, for enlistment of town and township leadership. At this stage, state should have leadership and quota acceptance in every county.

September—state activities are now concentrated on service: distributing publicity materials and campaign supplies, issuing a state bulletin on county progress, and booking speakers.

October—at campaign time the state has two big tasks: lending emergency help where help is needed, and trying to get weekly reports from the counties on campaign progress. (National headquarters is now quietly going mad, trying to get campaign reports from the states.)

November—state chairman thanks everybody, state executive writes his report, and state treasurer starts collecting the money.

Locally, the pattern on timing varies directly with the size of the community, all the way from the village that does the whole job in 24 hours to New York City, where no one has ever had time enough to organize thoroughly enough to cover the town completely.

In an average chest city, however, planning for the next year starts immediately after a campaign is completed. The campaign chairman is on the job seven months ahead, the top organization completed five months ahead, and all workers enlisted and trained at least three weeks in advance of the campaign opening. The average city starts soliciting advance gifts four weeks before the opening, and employee groups about two and a half weeks. Few cities try to run their chest campaigns in less than ten days, and the average campaign duration is about three and a half weeks.

Finally, on this problem of timing, the aim is a nice balance between starting too late and being ready too early. The dangers of starting too late are obvious, and much more frequently encountered. But it is also a great mistake to complete any part of a campaign organization more than a few weeks in advance of the time it is scheduled to function. In the one case, the grapes won't be ripe; in the other, they are more than likely to wither on the vine.

Quotas for Giving. Quotas, as already pointed out, should be established all the way down the line, from the state to the individual contributor. For unless there are standards for giving, the giving will not be proportionate, and unless the giving is proportionate you might as well forget the campaign, and merely run a "tag day."

There is no help for it, my friends; this is bound to get us involved in a slight case of statistics.

State standards we'll brush by. How they were established will be told in a later chapter; what they were will be found in the appendix. All we need say here is that the percentage for each state was fixed on estimated giving capacity, and not on sheer size or population.

Locally, it was found in the case of the National War Fund that about 60 per cent of the money came from organized chest cities, about 29 per cent from non-chest towns and rural areas, and about 11 per cent from New York City.

By groups, there was one general pattern for cities, and another for towns and rural areas.

In cities with populations of 25,000 or more (virtually all of which are "chest cities"), it was found that about a third of the money comes from the 100 largest givers, individuals and corporations, with almost half of this amount coming from the 10 largest givers. About another third comes from the 1,000 next largest givers, and the rest from everybody else. On source, it was found that 30 to 40 per cent of the money was contributed by corporations, and 20 to 30 per cent by organized employee groups.

In smaller cities and non-chest towns and rural areas, the best yardstick we found was to seek 60 per cent of the money from about 2 per cent of the population, with the 2 per cent group including those who were thought to be able and willing to give $25 or more.

Those are the key figures, but there are a few more findings that may be of general interest, and should be part of the record.

Any good campaign should produce at least one gift from each family in the community. (The average community chest, for example, gets about 28 contributions for each 100 of population.)

In soliciting employed groups, the "percentage of participation"— i.e., the percentage of contributors against the total number solicited —should be about 85, and is actually between 70 and 80. (High point in the war appeals was in Washington, D. C., with gifts from 91 per cent of 318,000 Federal employees solicited.)

The average individual, depending on the amount sought, should be solicited for some multiple of a day's pay; with the reservation, however, that the target should be a reasonable one, and should not be interpreted as a minimum below which no response is desired. Industrial workers are usually approached on some multiple of hours rather than days, and farmers in terms of commodities rather than wages. (In Minnesota's rural counties, for example, farmers in 1943 were urged to give the equivalent of a gross of eggs, or 35 pounds of pork, or five bushels of corn, or one day's cream checks.)

Finally, no one yet has found, or is likely to find, a satisfactory formula for giving by corporations. Many a fine scheme has been hatched, but the only plan that has been found workable is to get the largest possible gifts from the corporations which ordinarily set the pace, and let the others fall into line proportionately. (Incidentally, in most communities the best way to begin is to solicit the biggest bank, and then the rest of the banks that belong to the local bank clearing house. If the total given by the clearing house banks is at least 3 per cent of your local goal, you are then in good shape to start soliciting the rest of your local corporations. For the giving standard will be set, and many of the leading executives will know your story as a result of hearing about it at bank board meetings.)

Standards for Benefits. It used to be said that everyone wants to write a book, but in the early days of the National War Fund it often seemed to us that what everyone really wanted to do was to run a "benefit." Some of the plans were good, a few were highly productive, the great majority were strictly from dreamland, and almost all of them were full of dynamite—as potential threats to organized campaigns for proportionate gifts.

You can no more stop imaginative amateurs from having such ideas for raising money than you can keep weeds from sprouting in your garden. But you can and should establish certain standards for keeping the ideas under control.

These were the standards of the National War Fund:

The first and most important of the conditions under which the Fund would sanction a "benefit" plan was that all such plans had to be approved by local war chests or local committees of the Fund, wherever such local interests might be involved. This was sound in principle, and in practice killed off at least nine-tenths of the ideas.

Other standards set by the Fund were (1) that benefits should be associated with regularly scheduled events, and not with events specially arranged for benefit purposes; (2) that the auspices should be financially responsible, of well-established public repute, and activated by a genuine desire to help the Fund and its agencies; (3) that the role of the Fund must be that of a passive recipient only; (4) that no event, collection, or other enterprise in which the Fund was to share could charge more for tickets, services, or other *quid pro quo* than was usually charged; and (5) that under no circumstances would the Fund sanction or accept money from a benefit involving the sale of tickets or merchandise on the "remit or return" plan, or the employment of salesmen on a commission basis.

These requirements, plus a few analogous rules on projects of a commercial or quasi-commercial nature, were designed both to protect the general public and to preserve the principle of proportionate giving.

Cost Standards. Budget blindness can kill a fund-raising campaign before it even gets started, the usual trouble being that too many people have extemporized lifelong convictions on campaign costs in terms of percentage. "We can spend only 3 per cent," they say, or some other arbitrary percentage, without taking into account the size or complexity of the constituency to be covered, the amount to be sought, or the period of time involved.

The facts are that percentage costs vary inversely with the size of the goal and directly with time and the number of desired contributions. The result is that it may cost nothing at all to raise your quota in Elida, Ohio, and as much as ten per cent in New York City—as much as twenty per cent if you try to do it all by mail.

The cost of a fund-raising campaign should be estimated in terms of what has to be done, how much staff and how many tools are needed to do it, and how much time is involved. That takes planning, rather than guesswork, and good planning won't be helped by jumping to conclusions on percentages.

Most campaigns spend too little rather than too much. Most of the cost is involved in raising the last ten per cent of the money. And 'the most effective investment in campaign cost is competent staff.

If you remember that, you can throw the rest away.

METHODS

All that prologue may turn out to be longer than the play itself— the story of how the money for the National War Fund was actually raised. But for that we'll have no apology; the fundamentals of the prologue should have more lasting and widespread significance, and in themselves tell most of the story to be recited here.

Nationally, the campaign activity of the National War Fund was supplementary, and designed for no other purpose than to help local campaigns reach their goals.

The Division on Benefits and Special Promotions, under the direction of Robert F. Kelley, would have been justified for its police work alone. But as you will find when we start listing campaign results, the division also was responsible for raising significant sums of money through racing, baseball, and miscellaneous promotions. Committee, no; all we had, and all we needed, was Bob Kelley.

The rest of the national activity was centered in the Division of Special Services, for two years headed by Virgil Martin, in 1945 by George Hamilton, and in all three years backed and guided by a representative committee of chest laymen and executives under the chairmanship of T. L. Webster, chest executive at Columbus, Ohio. (This, incidentally, was a ready-made committee, in that it had been recruited in 1942 as a committee on campaign and finance for Community Chests and Councils, Inc., and later found itself cheerfully shanghaied by the National War Fund.)

The two words "Special Services," purposely vague at the outset for the reason that the division's functions were far from clear, came in time to embrace a number of supplementary activities.

Most important of these, certainly in terms of measurable results, was the solicitation of certain national corporations under a committee headed in the first two years by Irving S. Olds, chairman of the board of the United States Steel Corporation, and in 1945 by Edward L. Ryerson, the man you'll have to beat if you want to be Chicago's First Citizen.

With the exception of a relatively few corporations which by choice were accustomed to being solicited nationally, all of the corporations covered by this committee were assigned to it by local war chests, and always, for one reason or another, because the chest city in which the corporation in question had its home office thought a national approach would be more effective. The result of this selective process was a list of some 83 national corporations, comprising one or more leaders in a number of fields whose standard of giving would be helpful locally, and for the most part companies in three specific fields which were felt to be more interested in the war-related appeals than in the traditional story of local community chests; namely, railroads, oil companies, and motion-picture producers.

In each year these corporations were solicited during the summer, and in all cases in time for September board meetings, primarily so that the gifts could be cited as standards in October local campaigns, and incidentally because the National War Fund, at that time of the budget year, always needed the cash. Where the corporation wished its gift to be allocated, in terms of the amounts to be credited to the communities in which it had a special interest, was in all cases left to the wishes of the donor—a subject, incidentally, which has to do with as fine a hot potato as ever threatened to burn the hands of any so-called national campaign.

In addition to this direct solicitation, the National Corporations Committee sent each year to some 8,000 officers and directors of corporations doing a gross business of a million dollars or more a special pamphlet about the Fund, as a means of cultivating interest in advance of requests for gifts.

An analogous special service, but handled separately, was the task of persuading certain national corporations to adopt a permissive policy on payroll deductions for employee groups.

Chest experience had long since indicated that anyone is likely to give more on the instalment plan of pledges rather than in one cash gift, but that pledges in the large numbers common to industry were difficult and costly to collect—unless the company concerned would consent to do the work by authorized payroll deductions. And a number of companies, in 1943, still frowned upon such deductions, possibly because the idea in general resembled too closely the "checkoff" for union dues.

In 1943, the Fund approached 32 such national corporations and persuaded 12 to change their policy. In 1944, the score improved: 19 changes out of 30 corporations approached. In 1945, nine more corporations were prevailed upon to permit payroll deductions, making a three-year total of 40 companies, affecting the giving of some 2,000,000 industrial workers. The effect could never be measured accurately, but certainly was all to the good.

A third service, again affecting the results of local campaigns, was the establishment of more effective liaison with organized labor, not only with the big war relief committees of the A. F. of L. and the C. I. O., but also with a number of important "independent" unions. This is a whole subject in itself, to be covered in a later chapter.

Another service was liaison with Washington, involving arrangements from the White House down for directives and understandings by which Federal employees, and civilians employed in war plants and industries under Government control, could participate effectively in local campaigns. All of this was accomplished to excellent effect under Major General Philip B. Fleming, Administrator of the Federal Works Agency, appointed by President Roosevelt as government liaison representative with the National War Fund.

These, together with the cultivation of chain store groups and maintaining effective contact with other current causes on the national level, were the principal methods pursued by the Fund to help local campaigns reach their goals.

On the state level, there was little or no fund-raising activity as such, though a few states did find it advantageous to set up "Special Service" committees, comparable to the national plan. Theoretically, the state organizations might have solicited a second line of the larger corporations, comprising selected companies doing business on a state-wide basis. Practically, this idea never became anything more than an idea, for the reason that all such corporations were handled locally, by mutual preference. The states could and did preach sound technique, turn a helpful hand to local campaigns finding themselves in trouble, and act through their bulletins as a useful clearinghouse for exchanging local experience. But they sought to raise no money, even by the supplementary methods used nationally, except in one vital particular.

One of the basic principles of fund-raising, cited early in this chapter, is that there has to be a cushion against failure. And nationally, arranging for any such cushion is always difficult, if not impossible. We did, to be sure, show a "Contingent Fund" in our national budget, but this was designed under many a watchful eye to allow solely for the unforeseen needs of the member agencies, under the unpredictable conditions of war. We could hardly have added another five or ten million dollars to the budget, with no more explanation than that some states might not reach their goals. The states wouldn't have stood for it, and probably not the agencies.

On the state level, however, the states could do unto others what they wouldn't have done to them, by adding a cushion for local failures to the net state quota before apportioning the gross state quota to their counties. This was usually done, and in many a state meant the difference between success and failure. The method was good; we salute it, we recommend it.

And now here we are on the good old "local level"—the place where money is really raised. And the question is one we'd rather see referred to Mr. Anthony himself—"how was it done?"

See all those stars in the sky? They look alike, don't they? Yet we know they're all different. And that's the way it is with local method.

The choice, then, is between pointing back to the fundamentals of fund-raising and a dissertation on the basic methods employed by the average community chest. And we prefer the fundamentals; not merely because the dissertation would make a volume in itself, but because anyone can better understand what he already knows about techniques employed in any given community if he understands the basic elements of a campaign and some of the laws that govern campaign operation.

These things every successful campaign for the National War Fund had in common, regardless of the size or location of the community: active and influential leadership, devoted and well-informed volunteers, a sound plan, proportionate giving, and a community-wide atmosphere of enthusiasm and success.

Benjamin Franklin himself summed up the essence of method in the following advice to one of his friends:

. . . and, in the first place, I advise you to apply to all those whom you know will give something; next to those whom you are uncertain whether they will give anything or not, and show them the list of those who have given; and, lastly, don't neglect those who you are sure will give nothing, for in some of them you may be mistaken.

RESULTS

Getting ready for a fund-raising campaign, we have shown, is a matter of months, and raising the money a matter of weeks. Finding out how much has been raised, and collecting it, is likely to be a matter of years. This, at any rate, was the experience of the National War Fund.

Reports. The first difficulty, in any federated national effort, lies in getting accurate reports on the amount of money alleged to have been contributed. The theory is simple enough, but the actuality can be a nightmare of the first order.

Theoretically, the local treasurer notifies the county treasurer, the county treasurer sends a weekly report to the state treasurer, and each state then notifies national headquarters. This is all carefully explained in advance, in much fine prose, and easy forms are provided to insure uniformity in reporting, and to reduce the whole process to an easy routine.

But alas, it doesn't work that way, and for a number of baffling reasons.

Locally, you run into one set of difficulties in chest cities, and another in non-chest towns and rural areas.

In chest cities, some of which have definite agreements with the state committee and some of which have not, finding out how much money was contributed for your particular national cause, and how much the chest will actually pay, is a long and complex process. If, for instance, the chest goal was oversubscribed, it is morally certain that your quota will be paid in full. But will you share in the oversubscription? If the goal was reached to the even dollar (a mathematical improbability with astronomical odds against it) your quota will probably be paid, depending on whether the loss in collecting local pledges is within the usual margin set up for such shrinkage, in originally determining the chest goal. If the goal was not reached, you may or may not be paid your quota, depending on how much money the chest has in reserve funds, and most of all on the level of community ethics. In general, you will be wise to assume that you will not be paid your full quota, and that national causes will suffer a bigger loss than the chest's local agencies. In the average chest city, "charity begins at home" is more than an aphorism; it's almost a law.

But that isn't all. For it develops that certain key chests have rules and customs of their own, which lead to still more national confusion. One important chest city in the Middle West, for instance, regardless of quota, would pay the National War Fund only on proof of disbursements to the Fund's agencies, refusing any share of either the administrative expense or the contingency fund. Another key chest, on the Atlantic seaboard, took its own expenses out of the advertised quotas for the agencies, instead of including an extra item for expense within its total goal. Other chests were assumed by state committees to have taken the standard quota, without formal agreement, and were found later to have taken a smaller quota—perhaps without sharing in the state expense, often without sharing in the state safety factor.

One more problem in finding out how much the Fund was to receive from a chest campaign had to do with time. One of the biggest cities in the East, for example, would declare how much the Fund was to be paid on the basis of the amount of cash and pledges in hand on the last day of the formal campaign period. Post-campaign receipts, it was held, were solely for the local agencies. Happily, that type of reasoning was exceptional.

Finally, in nearly every chest campaign there was always a conflict between fact and "face." Understandably, in an annual effort based so largely on pride in the community, and with a sound tradition for keeping a campaign within advertised dates for opening and closing, any local chest wants to be successful, and is therefore likely to announce the biggest possible total on the last day—as close as possible to the campaign goal. For that reason, if the chest is short of its goal on actual cash and pledges, it includes an estimated sum for "anticipatories"—gifts reported to be on the way, but not in the hands of the chest auditors. All of this makes up the total that appears the next day in the local newspapers, and which the state committee, in its original innocence, is apt to note with comforting satisfaction. Only later, and too often after the state has used the newspaper total in its report to national headquarters, is it learned that there is another result, based on audited fact.

For all these reasons, there is reporting difficulty in both directions. The average chest is cautious in committing itself, and is therefore slow to report to the state. The state, in turn, anxious to reach its state quota, and under pressure from national headquarters to report regularly, is likely to report chest results on hearsay or newspaper evidence. The result nationally is that you never, or at least hardly ever, know where you really stand on how much has been raised for your cause by local chests.

In non-chest towns and rural areas, the reporting difficulty is of another kind. Not much of the result is in pledges, and there is seldom any problem of sharing campaign failure with local agencies. The main trouble is that too many local chairmen are like the fabled village postmaster who held the outgoing mailbag until it was full— they don't want to report at all until they can say that the goal was reached. Frequently, when the report is made, it is a gross figure on the total raised, and not the net figure after deducting local expense. The state learns that later, and still later national headquarters has to make one more revision in its estimated result.

And then, if you can stand just a little more gloom in the interest of historical objectivity, there is also trouble on the state level itself.

All the states are supposed to report to national headquarters at the close of each week. It was a good week at the National War Fund when we heard from 40 states.

Again, all reports were supposed to be net—the amount raised for the Fund after allowing for state expenses. A few state reports, even after three years, were found to be gross. Add to that the fact that campaigns for the Fund were not all held simultaneously in the Fall (Rochester in May, New England resorts in the Summer, Florida in January and February) and even Mortimer Snerd could understand why a nationally federated cause has to be just a wee bit coy in announcing at any given time how much money has been raised in its interest.

How the reports actually came in, with the evidence on how the law of diminishing returns works on the total, is shown by the accompanying chart.

In each year the reporting leveled off after 16 weeks from the public opening of the appeal, the total around the fourth and fifth week proved to be substantially half of the amount finally reported, and more than 90 per cent of the final total was reported at the end of the eighth week, or the halfway mark.

Collections. Getting reports was one thing, and collecting the money was another. The chart on collections will demonstrate in itself that there is a significant lag between reports and collections, both in terms of time and dollars. The reason for this is a little like the weather; you can talk about it, but you can't do much to change it.

Chests, for example, and for sound purposes, stress pledges rather than cash. Most chest campaigns, run in the Fall for agency budgets in the following calendar year, don't need much immediate cash and raise more money when gifts are paid in instalments. Their collections, therefore, are apt to extend over much of the following year.

For that reason, and also because of sound budget practice, most chests pay their agencies in regular instalments, often in twelve equal amounts. Which may be all to the good for local agencies, but makes plenty of trouble for an emergency cause such as the National War Fund, particularly when its own budget year ends September 30th, and more than ever in its year of liquidation.

During the war, of course, all chests received an abnormally high proportion of cash, because of the effect of the excess profits tax on corporate gifts, and called for many pledges over a period of weeks instead of months, because of the employee turnover in war industry. But that had little effect, as far as the National War Fund was concerned. Habit is strong, and cash could be invested in short-term Government securities, thus earning the chest a little interest and lending praiseworthy help to the war bond drives.

The biggest collection problem of all, however, was the sheer inertia of the deposited dollar—an apparently inherent characteristic which

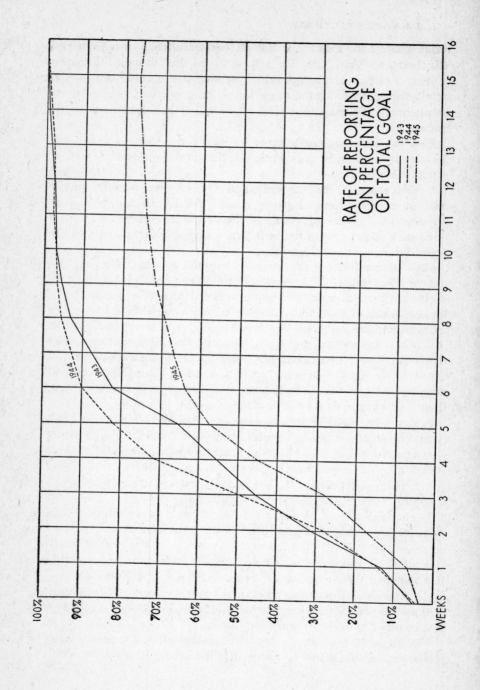

RATE OF REPORTING
ON PERCENTAGE
OF TOTAL GOAL

1943
1944
1945

1944
1943
1945

100%
90%
80%
70%
60%
50%
40%
30%
20%
10%

WEEKS

1 2 3 4 5 6 7 8 9 10 11 12 13 14 15 16

often seemed to us to make cold molasses look like so much quicksilver on a hot stove.

We should have been warned about this early in 1943, when fieldworkers first began to report the uncovering of moribund bank deposits that had been sleeping cosily ever since World War I—collections probably received after war work campaigns had closed their books, and meanwhile forgotten about by everyone, except some clerk, to whom it was nothing more than figures in the ledger.

Let it not be implied that there is anything discreditable about this. On the contrary, it probably reflects the sound and conservative practice of responsible banking, first of all in a local depository, possibly in a county depository, and finally in a state depository.

At each step, proper safeguards had to be taken to check out money only after proper certification, and only on multiple signatures. And some money had to be held at each level to meet delayed bills or claims, and to cover the initial expense of the effort for the following year. But when that happens in 48 states, and 43,000 communities, the lag can easily run into a large amount of money—literally millions in the first year of the National War Fund.

In any event, whatever the cause may be, you can put it down as a sure thing that the farther away a cause is from the ultimate contributor, and the greater number of stops there are along the line, the harder it is to collect the money, and the longer it will take to do it. This is true even in a single and closely controlled cause like the American Red Cross; it is all the more so in federation.

Net Results. Reflecting these difficulties in reports and collections, the figures for the three years of the National War Fund were as follows:

Year	Sought	Reported	Collected
1943	$125,000,000	$126,016,617	$121,066,294
1944	115,000,000	116,509,768	113,483,714
1945	115,000,000	86,703,934	87,020,804*
Totals	$355,000,000	$329,230,319	$321,570,812

The greatest shrinkage, it will be observed, was in the first year, due in large measure to the unexpected difficulties in getting net reports, and also to the fact that nearly all the states withheld funds for expenses in the following year, with many states also holding back oversubscriptions on their state quotas as a credit against the next appeal.

* Incomplete returns.

The final year reflects both the general letdown and confusion following V-J Day, and the difficulty of holding together the state and local machinery for collections throughout 1946.

Nevertheless, despite the shrinkage, the result still stands as an all-time record for federated fund-raising, particularly when it is taken into account that in the same federated effort there was raised for associated causes—mostly local chest agencies for health, welfare, and recreation—a three-year total of at least $422,462,824.

The joint harvest, therefore, not counting some $150,000,000 in the value of materials collected in gifts-in-kind campaigns (conducted by the agencies but financed by the Fund) was no less than $744,033,636. This is a mark not unlikely to stand for some little time, and without a doubt is substantially more than could have been raised by individual effort.

And now let's see where all that money came from.

Primarily, of course, it came from the 48 state war funds, New York City, and the District of Columbia. The accompanying table will show you the respective quotas, and the respective amounts paid to the National War Fund.

CONSOLIDATED STATEMENT OF STATE QUOTAS AND CONTRIBUTIONS RECEIVED FOR CAMPAIGN YEARS—1943-1944-1945
As of March 15, 1947

State	Combined Quotas 1943–1946	Total Net Amount Applied	Percentage
Alabama	$ 3,187,500.00	$ 3,138,750.00	98.47
Arizona	888,000.00	866,456.00	97.57
Arkansas	1,988,250.00	1,783,519.19	89.70
California	25,453,750.00	24,439,118.35	96.01
Colorado	2,697,250.00	2,743,034.18	101.70
Connecticut	7,850,000.00	6,425,544.65	81.85
Delaware	1,230,000.00	1,277,400.26	103.85
District of Columbia	3,357,325.00	3,008,200.00	89.60
Florida	3,774,500.00	2,201,773.69	58.33
Georgia	4,525,500.00	3,786,551.27	83.67
Idaho	1,083,000.00	1,085,165.35	100.20
Illinois	26,332,750.00	23,438,986.51	89.01
Indiana	8,564,665.00	7,281,665.02	85.02
Iowa	6,198,500.00	6,198,500.00	100.00
Kansas	3,537,000.00	3,236,252.03	91.50

State	Combined Quotas 1943-1946	Total Net Amount Applied	Percentage
Kentucky	4,063,250.00	3,817,315.55	93.95
Louisiana	3,739,750.00	3,433,471.46	91.81
Maine	1,964,250.00	1,646,772.19	83.84
Maryland	5,452,826.00	4,941,114.14	90.62
Massachusetts	13,600,000.00	11,737,478.06	86.30
Michigan	16,428,967.00	15,573,845.26	94.80
Minnesota*	6,874,160.00	6,843,249.11	99.55
Mississippi	2,144,000.00	1,865,638.52	87.02
Missouri	9,576,750.00	8,891,934.81	92.85
Montana	1,203,750.00	946,824.33	78.66
Nebraska	2,710,338.00	2,658,359.74	98.08
Nevada	388,000.00	426,340.21	109.88
New Hampshire	1,281,250.00	1,337,320.21	104.38
New Jersey	12,519,409.00	9,062,747.09	72.39
New Mexico	680,000.00	612,657.31	90.10
New York	61,064,079.00	50,596,242.03	82.86
North Carolina	5,313,750.00	4,907,564.59	92.36
North Dakota	1,030,000.00	1,032,592.79	100.25
Ohio	21,745,700.00	19,367,561.55	89.06
Oklahoma	3,636,796.00	3,254,525.70	89.49
Oregon	3,194,250.00	2,928,070.39	91.67
Pennsylvania	29,085,743.00	26,037,742.62	89.52
Rhode Island	2,350,745.00	2,126,019.00	90.44
South Carolina	2,112,750.00	1,827,151.20	86.48
South Dakota	1,063,843.00	958,684.63	90.12
Tennessee	4,522,416.00	4,522,416.00	100.00
Texas	13,184,700.00	11,931,301.71	90.49
Utah	1,131,500.00	1,096,539.72	96.91
Vermont	807,750.00	734,826.98	90.97
Virginia	5,188,851.00	4,960,782.01	95.60
Washington	5,106,000.00	4,761,195.57	93.25
West Virginia	2,851,500.00	2,456,248.99	86.14
Wisconsin	8,090,700.00	7,295,304.21	90.17
Wyoming	495,750.00	428,216.70	86.38
	$355,271,513.00	$315,928,970.88	88.93
Non-Quota and Miscellaneous Contributions		5,644,097.49	
Total Campaign Receipts		$321,573,068.37	

* Minnesota paid their 1943 and 1944 assigned quotas in full and paid $107,088.87 in excess of their accepted quota for 1945.

Not included in the quota system were the territories and certain groups of Americans resident in other countries. Here is their record:

	1943	1944	1945	Total
Alaska	$ 63,286.57	$ 75,231.25	$ 36,975.00	$ 175,492.82
Hawaii	452,621.88	393,804.76	249,242.75	1,095,669.39
Canal Zone	156,192.30	112,010.00	45,281.78	313,484.08
Puerto Rico	—	176,036.67	128,025.00	304,061.67
Virgin Islands	—	4,569.18	3,623.62	8,192.80
Totals	$672,100.75	$761,651.86	$463,148.15	$1,896,900.76
Costa Rica	—	$122,886.95	—	$ 122,886.95
Curacao (Aruba)	—	22,797.57	34,763.91	57,561.48
Peru	5,434.42	9,653.67	36.30	15,124.39
American committees in 10 other countries	5,724.91	2,467.38	8,033.03	16,225.32
Totals	$ 11,159.33	$157,805.57	$ 42,833.24	$ 211,798.14
GRAND TOTALS, outside the 48 states	$683,260.08	$919,457.43	$505,981.39	$2,108,698.90

Also not included in the quota system was a gift of $1,538,460 from the War Activities Committee of the Motion-Picture Industry, as a result of a collection for allied war relief in motion-picture houses throughout the country during the third week of January, 1943.

Included in the state quotas, because credits for the receipts were sent to the appropriate communities through the state war funds concerned, were the amounts raised by the National Corporations Committee, and by the Division of Benefits and Special Promotions:

	1943	1944	1945	Total
National Corporations	$8,281,662	$8,104,029	$8,070,576	$24,456,267
N. Y. Racing Associations	576,100	599,092	448,968	1,624,161
Season games, baseball	163,269	164,777	55,543	383,591
World Series	148,360	185,093	None*	333,454

Miscellaneous benefits, including the initial motion-picture collection, the $1,624,161 from racing, and the $717,045 from baseball, brought the total for the National War Fund to more than $4,000,000. Incidentally, the largest individual achievement in this field was by Bob Hope, who gave the Fund the royalties on his book, "I Never Left

* After V-J Day, and after Judge Landis.

Home"—a total at last accounts in excess of $155,000. (Bob probably doesn't know it, but that places him second only to John D. Rockefeller, Jr. as the biggest individual contributor to the National War Fund.)

BY-PRODUCTS

The by-products of the three campaigns with which the National War Fund was associated are of comparable interest and of even greater long-range significance.

What the war appeals did for the community chest movement is amazing enough in itself, in the number of chests, the number of chest contributors, and the amounts raised for purely local purposes.

In the last prewar year, 1941, the number of chest campaigns recorded by the statistical department of Community Chests and Councils, Inc., the national association of chests and councils of social agencies, was 632. The total raised, including modest quotas for the USO and a few other war-related agencies, was $104,575,890. (The total the year before had been $90,379,099.)

In 1944, for the chest year 1945, there were 772 chests reporting, and the total reached an all-time peak of $221,272,950. Even in 1945, after V-J Day, the number of chests had risen to 798, and the total amount raised was $197,048,839, or 89.6 per cent of total chest goals.

Giving by corporations went up from a prewar average of less than 30 per cent of chest goals to a war-time figure between 35 to 45 per cent. Giving by employee groups, around 20 per cent of chest goals in 1941, rose to a level between 25 and 35 per cent, with the percentage of employees contributing going up from a prewar average of 60 per cent to a war-time peak of 75 to 85 per cent.

In 1941, the average per capita gift to local chests was $1.83. By 1943, the figure was $3.11. Most significant of all, the number of contributors had increased by 25 per cent, and the amount raised for purely local purposes had gone up 40 per cent.

The chest movement made a great contribution to the success of the war-related appeals. But it should also be recorded that the war-related appeals never did the chest movement any lasting harm. The chests had the organization, and the war agencies had the appeal; as long as the war lasted, it was a winning combination.

Another significant by-product of the three years of war-time federation was the effect on the philanthropic point of view of American business. The prewar figures on the number of corporations giving, and the amounts contributed, rose like a rocket during the peak years of the war. But even as this is written, there is evidence that in the postwar period also, with the excess profits tax incentive gone, corporations will continue to be a much more significant factor in community campaigns.

Nationally, the figures for the first postwar appeal will not be available until after this volume has gone to press. Here, however, is a significant sampling from the experience in Cleveland during the community chest campaign concluded in November of 1946:

Group	No.	Community Chest 1941	Last War Chest 1945	Community Chest 1946	'46 % over '41
Banks	5	$ 53,750	$ 68,500	$ 62,000	15.3
Chains	6	36,400	53,000	47,800	31.3
Dept. Stores	5	60,000	118,350	118,350	97.9
Mfg.	23	218,300	523,400	390,410	78.8
Newspapers	3	67,500	88,000	76,000	12.6
Ore & Lake Int's.	6	55,100	111,000	84,500	53.3
Utilities	3	35,000	84,000	78,000	122.8
	51	$526,050	$1,046,250	$857,060	63.%

Organized labor too is in a different relationship to community problems of health, welfare, and recreation than it was before the war. In 1941, there were approximately 100 representatives of the American Federation of Labor on the boards and committees of local chests and councils. By 1946, the number was estimated at 6,500. The prewar representation of the C.I.O. was about 90, including representation on local chapters of the American Red Cross. By 1946, there were 1,410 C.I.O. representatives on chests and councils alone; 757 on chest boards in 333 industrial cities; 151 on local councils; and 498 on local boards of member chest agencies. This development, of course, was greatly to the advantage of campaign success, but was of far greater significance, in the minds of many, as a practical step toward the unity and understanding without which no community long can prosper.

We like to think too about the by-products in small towns and rural areas, such as the scout troops and nursing services which were made possible for the first time because of the readiness of the National War Fund to federate its appeal with local causes. There is as yet no record on how many such movements were given birth because of the war

NATIONAL WAR FUND, Inc.
CHART OF RECEIPTS AND DISBURSEMENTS
1943 - 1947

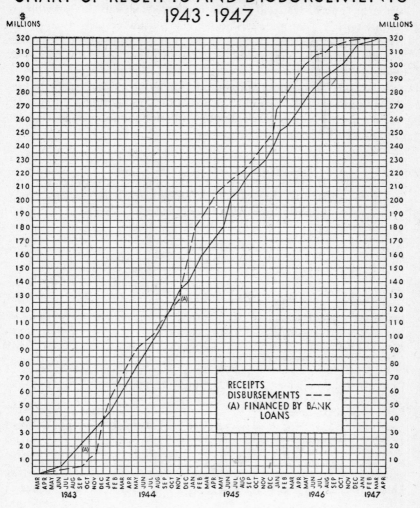

RECEIPTS ———
DISBURSEMENTS – – –
(A) FINANCED BY BANK
LOANS

appeals, but all of us, certainly, can hope that these are gains that will not be lost.

Finally, it is to be hoped that the universal response to a great effort made in time of war will lift the level of American philanthropy to permanently higher planes. The income tax law permits us to deduct charitable contributions within 15 per cent of our net taxable income, but the national average is only around 2 per cent by the figures we ourselves report.

It is still the greatest amount of money given to charity by any people in the world. But most of us in this predominantly Christian world still have a lot to learn about giving—for a current example, from our friends the Jews.

NATIONAL WAR FUND, INC.
SUMMARY SCHEDULE OF DISBURSEMENTS FROM INCEP-
TION AND ESTIMATE OF CASH REQUIREMENTS TO
COMPLETE AUTHORIZED PROGRAM
AS OF MARCH 15, 1947

	Total NWF Payments to March 15, 1947 (Including "Quota-Credits")	Estimated Additional Requirements (*)	Total (*)
Belgian War Relief Society	$ 2,207,299.63	$ 12,000.00	$ 2,219,299.63
British War Relief Society	5,944,033.18		5,944,033.18
Bundles for Britain	108,775.19		108,775.19
Catholic Welfare Conference, National	10,893,507.42	70,159.00	10,963,666.42
China, United Service to	32,379,196.19	154,944.67	32,534,140.86
Czechoslovakia, American Relief for	2,099,725.68	154,981.30	2,254,706.98
Denmark Relief, America	254,457.28		254,457.28
European Children, U. S. Committee for the Care of	296,751.58	76,953.62	373,705.20
Field Service, American	680,191.97		680,191.97
France, American Aid to	6,643,021.18	75,132.77	6,718,153.95
Greek War Relief Association	7,909,478.38	262,703.58	8,172,181.96
Holland, American Relief for	3,630,234.60	7,464.43	3,637,699.03
Italy, American Relief for	5,664,402.60	27,906.90	5,692,309.50
Lithuanian Relief Fund, United	808,370.88	4,500.00	812,870.88
Luxembourg, Friends of	295,410.47	5,096.60	300,507.07

	Total NWF Payments to March 15, 1947 (Including "Quota-Credits")	Estimated Additional Requirements (*)	Total (*)
Near East Foundation	802,101.34	12,000.00	814,101.34
Norway, American Relief for	2,527,637.95		2,527,637.95
Philippine War Relief	1,462,186.93	122,507.69	1,584,694.62
Poland, American Relief for	6,648,382.81	232,000.00	6,880,382.81
Prisoners Aid Committee, YMCA, War	9,597,044.29	152,118.13	9,749,162.42
Prisoners Aid, Inc., War	12,794.65		12,794.65
Refugee Relief Trustees	4,921,425.69	59,203.42	4,980,629.11
Russian War Relief	16,028,952.67		16,028,952.67
Seamen's Service, United	12,632,845.14	122,632.51	12,755,477.65
Social Hygiene Association, American	933,529.43	15,000.00	948,529.43
World Emergency & War Victims Fund, YWCA	1,655,244.30	6,728.81	1,661,973.11
World Student Service Fund	240,163.04		240,163.04
Yugoslav Relief Fund, United	3,051,682.65	106,635.08	3,158,317.73
Total Agencies (Exclusive of USO)	140,328,847.12	1,680,668.51	142,009,515.63
USO (United Service Organizations)	175,175,959.24	400,000.00	175,575,959.24
Total Agencies	315,504,806.36	2,080,668.51	317,585,474.87
Headquarters and Campaign Expense	2,142,867.07		2,142,867.07
Expense of Labor Campaign Committees	1,145,737.10		1,145,737.10
Liquidation Expense and Contingencies	381,908.49	146,212.51	528,121.00
Total	$319,175,319.02	$2,226,881.02	$321,402,200.04

* Subject to adjustments for commitments, refunds, income, etc., as disclosed in Auditors' reports—and for over- or underexpenditures of agencies now in liquidation.

Budget Office—National War Fund, Inc.—March 17, 1947.

VI

FROM DOLLARS TO DEEDS

Tracing the dollars you gave to the National War Fund, all the way from New York to their ultimate destination, might drive an accountant to strong drink, but would cause all the angels to smile.

The help you gave may have been in one or more of 126 countries and major geographical areas—in any of six continents, and may have aided any one or more of some 200,000,000 men, women, and children.

Perhaps it was your money that decorated the Christmas tree in some USO clubhouse in Alaska, that provided convalescent care for some torpedoed American seaman, that brought books or games to your own son in a Nazi prison camp, or sent an American ambulance driver up a Burmese jungle road. Or perhaps it was your money that put shoes on the bare feet of a Norwegian farmer, or saved some Greek child from starvation in the days before Athens was freed, by setting a table before him in the presence of his enemies.

Yours could have been any one of many millions of simple little acts of kindliness, the totality of which can never be measured, but the essence of which is just as human, and just as tangible, as the extra cake passed over an American back fence when a neighbor needs it.

Making deeds out of dollars on so broad a front, in face of such appalling need, and under all the strictures of war-time handicaps and regulations, was much more, however, than a matter of neighborly generosity. It was a task that called for sympathetic realism and an inescapable degree of rules and controls.

The basic policies governing the budgeting of the Fund have been outlined in Chapter II, "Rules of the Game." In this chapter, we shall try to picture for you how the budgeting process worked, and give you some idea of the consequent operations of the agencies themselves.

BUDGET PROCESS

There were people, and there was system, and it was the people who really counted.

72

Who the people were, you'll find in the appendix: a Budget Committee large enough to cover all the necessary hearings, devoted enough to give a great amount of time, and representative enough to insure a democratic cross-section in point of view. In the selection of the membership, consideration was given to geographical representation and public position, but most of all to the factors of budget experience and willingness to spend the necessary amount of time and energy.

Here were representatives of all three major faiths, of industry, banking, the law, foundations, community chests, and organized labor; none of whom, however, were special pleaders for any particular cause or agency. It was an experienced and well-balanced group, the deliberations of which often led to disappointment, but never to charges of unfairness or partiality. Incidentally, one of the reasons for this was that time was always taken to bring debate to unanimous agreement, with the result that the committee's ultimate recommendations were invariably approved by the Executive Committee of the board.

The system, laid down by the governing policy, was one of meetings, conferences, and reports; the meetings at quarterly intervals, and the conferences and reports going on month by month and day by day. The aims were in keeping with the Budget Committee's threefold responsibility: to recommend inclusion of agencies, to review and recommend budgets, and to supervise the distribution of allocated funds.

How agencies came to be included in the Fund was explained in Chapter II, as well as the general process by which budgets were screened in Washington, and reviewed in New York. For the record, however, let it be added here that the quarterly screening in Washington involved consultation with the President's War Relief Control Board, Lend-Lease, the Army, the Navy, the Treasury, State Department, UNRRA, the War Refugee Board, the Foreign Economic Administration, and often the American Red Cross. These consultations made it possible for the Budget Committee to approve any given agency project with assurance that the need was real, that the relief materials could be spared, found, and shipped, and that the purpose was within the framework of strategic policy and free from duplication by any other governmental or private relief agency. Many a project, incidentally, had to be modified or disallowed for failing to meet these initial requirements in Washington.

After the review in Washington, the certified projects were submitted to panels of the Budget Committee at two-day quarterly hearings in which another set of questions was always involved—the big question, invariably, being how to meet a mountain of need with a molehill of money.

The representatives of the agencies, to be sure, tried to temper their requests to the total of the funds available. Always and understandably, however, most of the agencies wanted more than could possibly be granted.

The total result, approximately, was a three-to-one mixture of pleasure and pain. It was a great satisfaction to the committee, for the three active years of the Fund, to approve budgets in the aggregate amount of $343,249,564. But no one enjoyed having to reduce agency requests in that time by $106,917,031. There simply wasn't enough money to go around.

Consequently, in its best judgment the committee had to decide between the relative urgency of the need in one area as against another, and between the relative priority of agency projects, keeping constantly in mind the principle that private aid was for emergencies or needs outside the scope of governmental or public funds, that programs had to be related to the cause of winning the war, and that projects had to be administered both without discrimination as to color, creed, race, or political belief, and in such a way as to permit proper accounting. Later, when the Allied forces had driven the Nazis back into Germany, the committee further modified budgets on the principle that relief priority should be given to areas recently liberated.

One of the necessary rules, once budgets had been determined, was that the agencies could not shift funds from one project to another, even though the total amount of its budget was unaffected. All such reallocations required further approvals from the President's War Relief Control Board and from the Budget Committee. This, of course, led to more multiple screening in Washington, and to endless conferences in New York.

These conferences, usually on a staff level, were an important and fruitful factor in keeping the budget process on an even keel and in an atmosphere of mutual goodwill and understanding.

Finally, the routine necessarily involved reports—reports from the agencies at regular intervals, on standard forms, to be examined and analyzed by the Fund's two budget comptrollers. Once a year, the Fund required an audited statement. Each month, the agencies were obliged to report their current position and to justify requests against budgets for the following month. Agencies were allowed reasonable advances against operating requirements, but were not permitted to build up stock-piles of relief supplies.

In this auditing process, all agency cash, accounts receivable, and inventories at the end of any fiscal year were considered as assets to be applied as reductions of gross requirements for the fiscal period following. Commitments were allowed as liabilities only if billed or shipped within, and applicable to, the prior period. Purchased supplies were considered inventory unless actually shipped abroad by the end of the fiscal period in question.

All of which was pretty tiresome to the agencies, and makes tiresome reading. But it kept things moving, and kept things under responsible control. It was therefore clearly in the public interest, even though of doubtful interest to the public.

One more bit of basic background, and then we'll move on. It should be recorded, we believe, how time dealt with the budget process. For the three active years of the Fund were not of equal duration.

In the first year, the agencies came into the Fund with actual and potential assets of almost $50,000,000. Gross budgets were approved for the calendar year 1943, and for the first nine months of 1944. Funds raised in the Fall of 1943, therefore, covered net requirements for 1943, and gross requirements from January 1 to October 1, 1944.

The second appeal, in the Fall of 1944, financed a period of exactly twelve months, from October 1, 1944, to October 1, 1945.

Originally, the budget for the third period was also to have covered exactly twelve months. At the end of hostilities, however, it was agreed that the appeal to be made in the fall of 1945 would be the Fund's final appeal, and that agency budgets should be stretched to cover the fifteen months ending December 31, 1946.

Two explanations are in order here. As nearly every local chest conducts its affairs on the basis of the calendar year, why did the Fund fix the end of its first fiscal period at the end of September, 1944? The reason was that $125,000,000—considered the ceiling from a fund-raising point of view—would stretch no further than that.

Similarly, why were the final budgets for the agencies stretched to fifteen months, instead of twelve? Here again, the reason was a practical one, having to do with the Fund's essential relationships with local chests. After V-J Day, the letdown was immediate. Quotas were in question, and even inclusion of the war-related appeals came into local chest debate. The problem of maintaining the budget at the original figure of $115,0000,000, and holding to the pattern of full federation, could be solved, we found, in only one way; namely, to stretch agency budgets for 15 months, and thus keep the agencies out of the area of separate fund-raising for the entire year of 1946. And this wasn't as hardhearted as it may sound, for the reason that the USO, the biggest agency of all, promptly reduced its monthly requirements as soon as the Japanese surrendered.

The three "years," then, were of some 16 months, 12 months, and 15 months; one more evidence of the risk in generalizations, and one more reason why there was rarely a dull moment in the budget work of the National War Fund.

THE STORY OF THE AGENCIES

So much for all the fine background: procedures which had to be set up in order to send your dollars fairly and swiftly to the points of greatest need, but which in themselves would never have brought a smile to the face of a tired G.I., a single meal to a hungry refugee, or a coat to the back of a shivering child. It was the agencies that turned the dollars to deeds, and thus accomplished the things you wanted done when you generously wrote those checks. So let's see what the agencies have to say for themselves, taking them one at a time, in the general categories in which they were classified.

SERVICE AGENCIES

Serving the armed forces and the merchant marine were five agencies: the USO, United Seamen's Service, American Field Service, and War Prisoners Aid, Inc.—all member agencies—and the American Social Hygiene Association, a participating service whose budget was affiliated with that of the USO.

USO. (Total approved budget, $181,181,827) Itself a federation of six national agencies,* plus the affiliated USO-Camp Shows, the USO had the task, from February, 1941 to December, 1947, of providing entertainment everywhere for the enlisted personnel of our own armed forces, and a multitude of other services—in all theatres except

---

* The Young Men's Christian Association.
  The National Catholic Community Service.
  The National Jewish Welfare Board.
  The Young Women's Christian Association.
  The Salvation Army.
  The National Travelers Aid Association.

the combat area in the war with Germany—which came to be known by nearly everyone as the G.I.'s "home away from home."

The USO conducted its own appeals in 1941 and 1942, and raised substantially $50,000,000. It was obliged to conduct its own final appeal in 1946 for its terminal budget of $19,000,000. The bulk of its service, however, was performed during the period of its affiliation with the National War Fund, with a peak of 3,035 clubs and other facilities at a monthly cost of $5,800,000, and with an average daily attendance of 1,000,000 at USO Clubs and Camp Shows.

Operations included clubs, mobile services, and troops-in-transit lounges in every state, and in Hawaii, Alaska, Newfoundland, the Antilles, Canal Zone, Brazil, and the Philippine Islands. Those served included both the armed forces and their visiting wives and families, and in war-time, industrial workers in some 200 overloaded communities. After V-J Day, service to industrial workers was discontinued, but extended to veterans in hospitals.

USO-Camp Shows played to as many as 700 audiences a day in all parts of the world, with its 6,000 troupers running up a record of more than 400,000 performances to a total audience of 202,000,000—a new mark for show business.

More than one and a half million volunteers worked for USO, giving more than 191,000,000 hours of service, a story told with captivating warmth by Julia Carson in her "Home Away from Home," published by Harper Brothers in the summer of 1946. But if you want still more detail, just ask one of those volunteers, or almost any returned G. I.

United Seamen's Service. (Total approved budget, $13,450,000) It was the fighting men who won the war, but it was ships that made the victory possible. This was the agency that served the men who manned the American merchant marine; the men who delivered supplies to our Allies and later took our armies to the European and the Pacific theatres of war, supplied them, and brought them home. The merchant seamen ran the gauntlet to Murmansk and the islands of the Pacific, and defied the U-boat packs when the sinking of ships was at its height.

Thanks to you, U. S. S. operated 165 rest, medical residence, recreation, and personal service facilities for our merchant seamen in 93 ports of the six continents—22 in the United States and 71 overseas. The Army and Navy gave this work their highest praise; both General Eisenhower and Admiral Nimitz have testified to its invaluable contribution to victory.

The U. S. S. residential clubs have been a "home away from home" for the seamen who "shared life and death, attack and victory" with the men of the armed forces.

American Field Service. (Total approved budget, $1,008,876) More than 1,000,000 sick and wounded were carried in the ambulances of the American Field Service, attached to British and French Armies in the European theatre, the Middle East, North Africa, India, and Burma. Enlisted from 45 different states, 2,196 American drivers served voluntarily for enlistment periods of 18 months, and more than doubled the service record of World War I.

The agency became a member of the National War Fund in the spring of 1944, after raising its own funds for more than four years. It was one of the first agencies to begin to liquidate its affairs as soon as hostilities ceased.

War Prisoners Aid. (Total approved budget, $10,240,188) Life in a prison camp is something even a former prisoner of war can rarely explain adequately. Cut off from home, cut off from news, without privacy, without adequate food and comforts, and worst of all, without freedom, a prisoner faces endless hours of dreary labor and stagnant idleness.

Under the provisions of the Geneva Convention of 1929, the function of War Prisoners Aid was to bring to all prisoners of war—enemy prisoners in Allied hands as well as Allied prisoners in the hands of the enemy—a wide variety of recreational, educational, and spiritual services, under the direction and supervision of neutral visitation.

Your money bought books, games, musical instruments, hobby materials, equipment for religious services, and a variety of other similar aids, and sent them promptly to prison camps through neutral and responsible auspices. The Y.M.C.A. alone, in thirty countries, served more than 5,000,000 prisoners, largely through Y.M.C.A. secretaries from Sweden and Switzerland. Similar services under the auspices of the National Catholic Welfare Conference, with a total budget of $2,056,000, were rendered through the Swiss Catholic Mission.

This was the fight against idleness, boredom, stagnation, and despair; a fight you helped to win when you gave to the National War Fund.

American Social Hygiene Association. (Total approved budget, $1,120,000) The peace-time program of this agency was stepped up sharply to meet the war-time emergency, broadening all its educational activities both for members of the armed forces and for war workers, intensifying its law-enforcement program, and extending its community services on a much broader front in an all-out attack on prostitution and venereal disease.

Gains made by the agency during the war should also bear continuing fruit in peace-time. The Association from 1943 through 1946 made 2,159 surveys of prostitution conditions in 1,736 communities; stimulated educational programs in these and many other communities and among the armed forces; distributed 7,900,000 pamphlets; exhibited over a thousand films and displayed 267,000 exhibits and posters.

Under ASHA guidance, more than a score of states strengthened laws against prostitution, enacted premarital and prenatal laws, or amended existing laws. Field service representatives, working from six regional Association offices, promoted the national VD Control program by establishing liaisons between citizen groups and military and public health authorities, by initiating citizen action in communities, and by organizing affiliated social hygiene societies. An industrial educational program enlisted management, employees, and trade-unions throughout the country and included publication of articles in house organs and union papers with a total circulation of more than three million, as well as the sponsored distribution of almost two million tabloid leaflets to employees. Association leaders joined with Federal agencies in a "team plan," which visited and continues to visit selected communities with the objective of organizing Stamp Out VD programs, and establishing affiliated social hygiene groups. Association-sponsored Social Hygiene Day meetings were held annually in thousands of cities and towns.

RELIEF AGENCIES

In the field of foreign relief, the extent of assistance provided by agencies of the National War Fund is difficult to estimate. At the last computation, in February, 1946, these agencies had provided 40,894,000 pounds of food, 99,400,000 pounds of clothing, and 67,216,000 pounds of medical and other supplies.

In addition to the food, clothing, and medical supplies, aid given the people of our Allied nations included maintenance of orphanages, homes, hostels, clinics, nurseries, and rest centers; child-care, nursing, and medical instruction and training; transportation and shelter for displaced persons, refugees, and returned prisoners of war.

At one time or another, 23 agencies were included in the Fund as member agencies or participating services. Each has a long record and

an impressive story of its own. Our aim here, therefore, is merely to
review some of the high lights.

Belgian War Relief Society. (Total approved budget, $2,317,030)
Following the liberation of Belgium, this agency shipped approximately
9 million pounds of relief supplies, including 6,265,339 pounds of
clothing, 1,450,817 pounds of food, 988,979 pounds of medical supplies and drugs, and 270,730 pounds of household equipment.

As in the case of other liberated countries, it was found that the
Belgians not only needed clothing, but even lacked the needles and
thread for sewing patches and buttons, and the tools with which to
mend their shoes. In addition, therefore, to sending more than a half
million pairs of shoes, the agency sent a great supply of shoe repair
kits. And in addition to sending clothing, underwear, socks, and layettes, the agency found it necessary to send sewing machines, sewing
kits, and more than 12,000 pairs of ordinary knitting needles. The
food sent, mostly for women and children, was to supplement rigid
diets of the period immediately following the liberation.

Relief supplies were distributed under the direct supervision of the
Society's own Committee in Belgium, which has accounted in full for
all supplies shipped.

British War Relief Society. (Total approved budget, $8,686,874)
One of the first American agencies to be organized after the outbreak
of the war, the British War Relief Society supplied, equipped, and
maintained 316 ambulances, surgical units, and first-aid vehicles,
operating on a 24-hour service from 27 stations throughout the British
Isles. It supplied 1,000 mobile feeding kitchens and food convoys,
serving fire fighters, rescue crews, and bombed-out civilians, wherever
German bombs brought disaster.

It equipped and maintained 200 homes and hostels for bomb-
shocked, injured, and orphaned children, and a number of homes for
aged and infirm people rendered homeless by air attacks. It provided
equipment for air-raid shelters, Christmas toys for homeless children,
hundreds of thousands of packets of vegetable seeds for British gardens,
cash grants for many thousands of families, clothing for those who
had been bombed out or torpedoed, and 22 clubs in the principal ports
of the United States and Canada for the recreation of the British
Merchant Marine and the Royal Navy.

Included in the budget of the British War Relief Society was the
budget of Bundles for Britain, administratively a separate agency, but
equally devoted to the huge task of providing emergency relief for the

British people, and principally for the British children, during the days when Britain bore the brunt of Germany's attacks by air.

Both the British War Relief Society and Bundles for Britain, in a gesture that will be long remembered, voluntarily withdrew from the final appeal of the National War Fund, to enable the Fund to concentrate its final resources on relief in countries which had been liberated by the Allied victory. By American standards, the British people still needed our aid, but felt that the need elsewhere should have priority.

United Service to China. (Total approved budget, $32,699,559) To help the Chinese people help themselves, and to sustain Chinese faith in the United States at a time when the tide of Japanese arms was at its height, this agency succeeded in bringing direct aid to more than 22 million of the Chinese people.

Food, shelter, and clothing were provided for 4 million refugees; care was given to 163,514 children, medical service for 3,145,433 civilians, and surgical and medical service for 13,500,000 Chinese soldiers. In its medical and surgical help for the Chinese army alone, sending back to active service hundreds of thousands of those who might never have fought again, this agency made tangible contributions to the military victory. But of more long-range significance, it has contributed greatly to the future of China by granting emergency subsidies to 309,676 students and professors, who otherwise could not have carried on, and trained more than 100,000 professional people in the administration of health and welfare programs. In ways such as this, the agency kept open the historic highways of friendship between the people of China and the people of the United States.

American Relief for Czechoslovakia. (Total approved budget $2,397,023) From July, 1944 to October, 1946, the period during which this agency concentrated its program, American aid was extended to more than 300,000 of the liberated people of Czechoslovakia. Supplementary food was provided for 70,000 of the most needy school children, for 34,000 other boys and girls in 616 summer camps, and 5,000 in orphanages and institutions. Clothing was distributed to 207,330 children and adults, and $422,728 worth of medical equipment supplied for hospitals which had been stripped of all their facilities by the Nazis.

In all, the agency shipped 1,297 tons of food, medical equipment, soap, clothing, blankets, and shoes, including 915 tons of milk, eggs, and cocoa, 30 oxygen cabinets for premature babies, 8 complete dental units, and 20 complete sets of X-ray equipment, sufficient to examine the entire population for tuberculosis. It is significant that one mobile X-ray truck, sent out to examine the children, found 60 per cent of those in devastated Silesia afflicted with the disease.

America Denmark Relief. (Total approved budget, $316,595) The Germans conquered Denmark, but never the Danes. Knowing this, and knowing the German record for looting the people of the occupied countries, American friends of Denmark organized this agency both to help Danish refugees, and to be prepared for the day of liberation; raising nearly $150,000 for the purpose before the agency came into the Fund.

But when liberation came so swiftly, and it was found that the people of Denmark were relatively better off than the people of Holland and Belgium, the Danish people themselves suggested the withdrawal of the Danish appeal, with the result that this agency did not participate in the final appeal of the National War Fund.

U. S. Committee for the Care of European Children. (Total approved budget, $1,071,835) The function of this agency, established in 1940, was to provide American haven and care for babies and children brought here from the bombed and bomb-threatened areas of Europe and the British Isles. Under conditions of responsible control, many hundreds of children were brought to good American homes, and given the kind of care and security which meant life itself to many, and which in years to come should help build lasting goodwill.

American Aid to France. (Total approved budget, $7,325,300) June 6, 1944 opened the path for the invasion of France by the Allied armies, and also opened the channels for American relief to the French people. After it became possible to send such relief, this agency shipped 12 million pounds of clothing, bedding, baby accessories, toilet goods, food, and medical and surgical supplies, in aiding more than two million French people in areas which had suffered most from the war. The agency operated disaster units and mobile canteens for homeless populations, helped the families of Resistance members who had been shot or deported, carried basic supplies to people who had lost all their household possessions, provided medicines and specialized foods to combat malnutrition among approximately 300,000 children and adolescents, and founded general welfare centers in devastated regions. Gifts-in-kind were valued at $400,000 per year, and an estimated $500,000 worth of merchandise per year went direct to more than 7,000 children through package adoptions.

More than 11,000 volunteers, in some 300 American communities, helped prepare the clothing and other comforts sent to France.

Greek War Relief Association. (Total approved budget, $14,049,-043) In the dark days of the German occupation, this agency is credited with having saved at least one-third of the Greek people from annihilation from starvation and disease, through the trans-blockade program which for three years sent 14 Swedish ships on 101 Atlantic crossings, carrying 700,000 tons of food and relief supplies for distribution to the Greeks alone, under the strict supervision of the International Red Cross.

Following the liberation of Greece in October, 1944, the Association gave special emphasis to projects in the fields of public health and child welfare, operating 474 clinics in every section of Greece, and sending 40 mobile medical units to remote mountain areas and badly devastated regions and villages. During this period, the Association maintained 2,000 child-feeding centers, caring for more than 1,200,000 children between the ages of two and fourteen, as well as 29,000 pregnant women and nursing mothers. The agency provided training and artificial limbs for disabled Greek veterans, X-ray units in Athens and Salonika for examination for tuberculosis, 12,000 farm animals to start restocking the farms of Greece, and more than 8 million garments and shoes for general distribution.

Nowhere in Europe did war strike harder, and nowhere has American aid striven harder to send commensurate help.

American Relief for Holland. (Total approved budget, $4,260,887) Prior to the liberation of Holland and dating back to its organization in 1940 as the Queen Wilhelmina Fund, this agency was obliged to confine its program to Dutch refugees. Liberation brought the opportunity for direct relief, and disclosed an appalling emergency. There followed one of the swiftest and most effective relief programs in the history of the Fund, high-lighted by flying into Holland "predigested" protein hydrolysates, without which Dutch children were found to be unable to assimilate food.

During the two years in which the agency concentrated its relief program for Holland, 14,000,000 pounds of relief supplies were shipped to help provide the clothing, food, soap, medical supplies, and household equipment by means of which the self-reliant Dutch people got back on their own feet. With much of the land flooded, most of the industries wrecked, thousands of homes stripped of furniture and equipment, the liberated Dutch people were without shelter and heat, and needed help immediately and in almost every form. This agency's program was a triumph of sound planning and fast operation, aided by the expert cooperation of responsible agencies in Holland itself.

American Relief for Italy. (Total approved budget, $5,855,000) Coming into the Fund early in 1944, after the Italian surrender in the previous September, this agency brought emergency help to more than 10 million men, women, and children. Through the National Committee for the Distribution of Relief in Italy, comprising representatives of the Italian government, the Vatican, the Italian Red Cross, and the Italian General Confederation of Labor, the agency was able to distribute 49,796,854 pounds of relief materials, free from the cost of distribution, and with the assurance that relief would be given regardless of creed or politics.

The agency provided one pint of milk a day for 150,000 undernourished Italian children, sent insulin to thousands of diabetics, and medical supplies to 350 hospitals.

United Lithuanian Relief Fund of America. (Total approved budget, $859,000) The program of this agency was directed primarily at the refugee problem, and only incidentally toward relief in Lithuania itself.

Aid was given to 75,000 Lithuanian refugees in Europe and South America, while to Lithuania itself it was found possible to send some medical supplies, clothing, and shoes for the civilian population, and equipment and clothing for some 800 children housed in four children's homes.

In all, for Lithuanian victims of the war who could be reached, the agency sent some 227,000 pounds of special supplementary foods, clothing for some 70,000 men, women, and children, shoes for 42,000 refugees, and 12,000 pounds of school supplies for more than 8,000 children. A substantial part of the program was providing cash assistance in the amount of $522,000 for orphans, widows, the sick or aged, and others temporarily in distress as a result of the war.

Friends of Luxembourg. (Total approved budget, $463,833) After the liberation of Luxembourg, this agency sent 347,477 pounds of clothing, 427,686 pounds of food, and some 33,000 pounds of medical supplies. In all, including 125,000 pounds of soap and approximately 800 blankets, the agency sent to Luxembourg nearly 1,000,000 pounds of relief supplies to the people who suffered the German invasion and occupation, and who with the Belgians took the shock of the last major German counterattack, in the Battle of the Bulge.

Near East Foundation. (Total approved budget, $884,186) As a participating service, with its budget channeled through the Greek War Relief Association, the Near East Foundation was financed by the National War Fund only for that portion of its program which had to do with Greece. In operation since World War I, the agency had the staff and the experience to supplement effectively the larger program of the Greek War Relief Association, by caring for crippled children in Athens, conducting centers for the medical care and the special feeding of some 2,000 children, by supplying clothing and medical care for the children of Greek soldiers killed in the war, and by operating a public health program on the Marathon Plain and in Macedonia. The agency also handled a significant volume of case work among Greek families broken up by the German occupation, and was able to help improve the livestock crisis in Greece through an artificial insemination program conducted in cooperation with Cornell University.

American Relief for Norway. (Total approved budget, $3,375,000) Organized in Chicago just ten days after the German invasion of Norway, this agency was fortunate enough not to be obliged to wait for liberation of the country before starting its program of direct relief. Through the aid of the Red Cross, a special Swedish committee of its own in Stockholm, and through the effective Norwegian underground, the agency was able to reach Norwegian school children with the equivalent of 18 million pints of fluid milk. It also found it possible to ship in food packages, medical supplies and medicines, aid for the families of those who had been executed or put in concentration camps, shoes for thousands of Norwegian prisoners of war in Germany, and books for Norwegian student prisoners, and aided a significant number of Norwegian refugees in Sweden. All of this was done while the Germans still occupied Norway.

After V-E Day, the program was stepped up by the shipment of a great variety of needed supplies, for distribution by an official organization, with 1,300 local aid stations all over Norway. These shipments comprised medicines, hospital equipment, new clothing, garments and layettes for children, shoes, boots, galoshes, and other essentials.

The agency also collected and sent to Norway some 2,309,700 pounds of used clothing, at an estimated value of $3,464,550. This additional program, though its expense was covered by the National War Fund, was made possible by thousands of volunteer workers.

Characteristic of the independent spirit of the Norwegians and their friends in the United States, the agency liquidated its relief program as soon as the situation in Norway was past the point of emergency.

Philippine War Relief (of the United States). (Total approved budget, $1,688,090) Relief for the Philippines moved directly behind the liberating forces of the United States Army, with an emergency program designed primarily to supply civilians with desperately needed household commodities, medicines, and clothing. Household and sewing kits, soap, tooth brushes, tooth powder, sewing machine needles, and comfort kits were supplied in large quantities. Over 4,000 cases of medical supplies and hospital equipment were shipped.

As garments usually made available through clothing collections in the United States are not suitable for the Philippine climate, the agency arranged for the production of 450,000 garments prepared especially for the purpose. In addition, however, approximately 5,000 volunteer sewing groups, mostly attached to churches and other societies in practically every state, made and remade upwards of 1,000,000 garments.

The function of the agency was chiefly to fill the interim need for supplementary relief, until official instrumentalities had a chance to institute broad-scale measures for rehabilitation and reconstruction. After liberation and early in 1946, 17 traveling clinics were organized to give medical, dental, and nursing care to the people in the provinces who suffered especially from diseases caused by starvation and privation due to the war. The clinics are manned by Filipino doctors, dentists, nurses, and social workers. They give treatments, dispense medicines, distribute clothing, conduct group and family instruction in nutrition and home care of sick; they also deal with problems of rehabilitation.

Fully 1,500,000 individuals benefited from the services of the mobile missions up to December 31, 1946. This work will be continued throughout 1947 largely by means of funds already allotted by the National War Fund in the 1946 budget.

American Relief for Poland. (Total approved budget, $9,021,400) During the last three years of the war, American Relief for Poland sent an average of 10,000 packages a month to former Polish soldiers held in German prison camps, provided clothing and medicines for thousands of Polish refugees in Africa, India, and the Near East, contributed substantially to the Polish Red Cross for the maintenance of clinics and convalescent homes for members of the Polish armed forces, and helped purchase and maintain the Paderewski Hospital at Edinburgh. The agency also financed an educational program for former Polish soldiers interned in Switzerland, and was able to send medicines and drugs into Poland during the German occupation through arrangements with the American Red Cross.

Direct relief for Poland itself was deferred so long, both by the German occupation and by conditions imposed after Russia moved in, that the National War Fund actually increased this agency's budget in the last year of the Fund, at a time when all but one of the other budgets had to be drastically curtailed. Instead of reducing the budget for Poland, in light of the results of the final appeal in the fall of 1945, the budget for American Relief for Poland was increased by $884,032.

Refugee Relief Trustees. (Total approved budget, $5,384,880) This agency represented a merger brought about by the Budget Committee of the National War Fund, in order to insure a unified program on relief for refugees, the agencies thus brought together comprising the American Christian Committee for Refugees, the International Rescue and Relief Committee, and the Unitarian Service Committee.

Under the merged program, relief for refugees was administered without regard to nationality, race, or creed, and was extended to refugees in some 30 different countries.

From the time the merger was made effective, in 1943, until the three agencies decided to go their separate ways in September, 1946, aid was extended to more than 200,000 displaced Europeans.

In view of the limitless nature of the need, and of the other work done in the field by private and governmental instrumentalities, the aim of Refugee Relief Trustees was to provide primarily for emergency situations which could not be covered in any other way.

Because of the acuteness of the refugee problem following V-E Day, and the consequent opportunity to perform services made possible only by the German surrender, the budget for this agency, like the budget for Poland, was increased by more than a million dollars in the last year of the National War Fund.

Russian War Relief. (Total approved budget, $16,191,088) This agency, later known as the American Society for Russian Relief, was a major participant in the National War Fund in 1943 and 1944, but withdrew from the Fund in the summer of 1945, and did not, therefore, participate in the proceeds of the final appeal. During the two years of its membership in the Fund, the agency shipped nearly $46,000,000 worth of relief supplies, including millions of pounds of clothing, seeds for replanting devastated farm lands, and medical supplies, and sent the Russian people a vast quantity of essential household items such as needles, pins, thread, and soap.

In addition to the supplies purchased with cash obtained from the National War Fund, Russian Relief collected millions of dollars worth of gifts-in-kind: used American clothing, blankets, household goods, seeds, watches, and many other related types of articles.

The total program of Russian Relief contributed substantially to the Allied victory, through material aid to the USSR and through encouraging a better understanding between the peoples of the two countries by means of friendly and nonpolitical aid.

War Relief Services — National Catholic Welfare Conference. (Total approved budget, $11,120,162) Under the rules of the National War Fund, this agency operated as a participating service, its budget heard as a separate unit but with the actual funds channeled through the member agencies representing the country or the function in which War Relief Services was to operate. The result was that this agency was integrated more closely with the operations of the other agencies in the National War Fund than any other, both in problems of administration in the United States, and in the conduct of relief projects in all the countries served.

All together, War Relief Services reached into 41 different countries, and provided an almost limitless program of relief and rehabilitation, ranging from morale-building activities for prisoners of war to the provision of food, clothing, and medical supplies for refugees and the homeless.

Because it was able to utilize the indigenous channels of the church, the agency was able to move swiftly and at a low cost, often being the first agency to reach the point of need, and yet committed everywhere to providing aid without regard to color or creed. The scope of its program was so vast, and the nature of its services so varied, as to make a brief summarization impossible. The agency was everywhere, with aid of all kinds, and set an enviable record for competence and economy.

World Emergency and War Victims Fund of the Y.W.C.A. (Total approved budget, $1,696,168) A participating service rather than a member agency, this organization conducted a supplementary program aimed particularly at helping women and children. In China, India, the Middle East, Great Britain, Europe, Southeast Asia, and Latin America the agency helped provide temporary and mobile relief equipment, emergency shelters and hostels, and in some cases sent American personnel to help administer emergency programs. In these and other ways, the Y.W.C.A. helped 2,353,500 people in some 26 countries, both with personal services and urgently needed relief supplies.

World Student Service Fund. (Total approved budget, $249,981) This agency was associated with the National War Fund for the first year only. Its aim was to provide books and study materials for student prisoners of war and interned students, and to provide work relief, food, clothing, and medical supplies for refugee students. Its work was international, nonsectarian and nonpolitical, and reached college and university students in some 17 countries.

United Yugoslav Relief Fund of America. (Total approved budget, $3,831,506) Yugoslavia was one area in which the President's War Relief Control Board was unable to bring about a unification of American relief. This agency, however, chosen as the group to be affiliated with the National War Fund, was able to plan and carry out a major program in the areas of direct relief and public health work. While Yugoslavia was occupied by the Germans, the agency's program was concentrated largely on relief for Yugoslav refugees and on parcels for Yugoslav prisoners of war. After it became possible to ship to Yugoslavia, the agency sent nearly 500,000 pounds of new and used clothing, 31,000 pairs of shoes, 31,816 medical and sanitary kits, 150,000 food parcels, as well as a large supply of such necessary household equipment as needles, thread, buttons, and safety pins. Of more long-range significance, the agency was able to institute a general public health program designed to meet both the immediate emergency and the necessary rehabilitation of medicine and nursing in Yugoslavia itself. Despite the political tensions involved, the agency held consistently to its policy of administering relief without regard to race, religion, or political belief.

COOPERATING ORGANIZATIONS

Though none of the money contributed to the National War Fund was channeled through either of the two labor organizations, both the A. F. of L. and the C.I.O. were active sponsors for special relief projects in a number of countries, both in Europe and in the Far East.

Originally, each of the two labor organizations had intended to conduct its own fund-raising campaign, principally among union members (though the C.I.O. also intended to solicit corporations with union contracts), for the purpose of financing relief programs in which American organized labor had a traditional interest. After the two labor committees came into the National War Fund, in the interest of war-time unity, they both gave up their independent fund-raising and also yielded the prerogative of administering relief funds and programs. Instead, each agency sponsored a number of special projects, so that labor could be put in the position of saying to its own adherents in the United States that these were causes to which union members should contribute freely and generously. It is worth emphasizing, in light of misconceptions which developed later, that neither of the labor committees was in the category of a member agency or a participating service, and that neither handled relief funds as contributions or disbursements at any time.

Projects thus sponsored by the Labor League for Human Rights of the A. F. of L. and by the National C. I. O. War Relief Committee, covered some 13 countries, and involved a total expenditure by the agencies of the National War Fund in the amount of $10,105,500. (Amount included in various agency budgets, noted on previous pages.)

These projects involved relief supplies, public health programs, homes for crippled children, youth hostels, subsidies for hospitals and sanitariums, and a considerable volume of cash relief for members of the underground in occupied countries.

Interestingly enough, the A. F. of L. estimates that members of its unions contributed some 140 million dollars to the National War Fund, to the associated community chest campaigns, and to the American Red Cross. The C.I.O., in turn, records the fact that its members, from 1942 to the end of 1945, contributed to these same causes at least 125 million dollars.

Whatever the exact figures may have been, members of American labor unions contributed far beyond the measure of the projects in which the A. F. of L. and the C.I.O. expressed a special interest.

*　*　*

All of this, admittedly, makes a sparse and barren tale; sparse because the canvas is far too big for the picture, and barren because statistics have no life.

You can better visualize the deeds done by your dollars, perhaps, by trying to put yourself in the place of a Dutch mother whose child's life was saved by a drug flown from America—a Czech whose first good meal in years was dropped in an American parachute—a diabetic in Naples brought out of her coma by insulin from across the Atlantic— a Chinese soldier saved by a blood bank flown over "the Hump"—a Russian soldier relieved from agony by an anaesthetic from Indianapolis—a prisoner of war with something constructive to do for the first time in many weary months—any G.I. away from home.

The conclusion you can fairly draw is that your deputies in decency— the agencies of the National War Fund—did a swift, comprehensive, and intelligent job in extending your aid wherever it was needed most.

And you can also feel assured that it was done in a way both Jefferson and Lincoln would have heartily approved—without regard to race, creed, color, or political belief.

This was the American genius for efficiency and economy, linked with the American ideal of the good neighbor.

We were in a big hurry to win a great war, but we also found time to pause on the road to Jericho.

VII

RELATIONSHIPS

On a global basis, and in time of war, the role of the good Samaritan, as we have seen, involved planning, leadership, organization, publicity, salesmanship, budgeting, and agency programs. It also involved a series of complicated relationships.

As the main business at hand was the winning of the war, the business of the National War Fund had to be related at every step to the primary requirements of victory. First of all, therefore, through the President's War Relief Control Board, it was essential to establish effective liaison and understanding with official Washington.

WASHINGTON STORY

It was like finding your way through a mine field. Security regulations necessarily blocked off many a story that could have been told about the USO and United Seamen's Service. The Geneva Convention, with its reciprocal agreement on the care and treatment of prisoners of war, meant that this subject had to be handled with all the kid gloves of protocol—particularly at the time when Japan held so many Americans, and we had captured so few Japanese.

There were also the little matters of blockade restrictions, censorship of mails and cables, rules on foreign transfers of funds, limitations on passports and transportation, and the quantitative control of purchases and exports of such essentials as medicines, food, and clothing. And then again, from a fund-raising point of view, there were questions on the extent to which Federal employees would be urged to contribute to local war fund campaigns.

The wonder is, under all these pressing circumstances, that the Washington relationships were as effective as they were: usually swift when long delays might reasonably have been excused, and always fair when one might have expected some human display of departmental prerogative.

The fact that the liaison worked so well is to be attributed primarily to Franklin D. Roosevelt: first, because his appointment of the War Relief Control Board lifted the whole problem of voluntary war relief above the level of partisanship and bureaucracy; second, because he made it eloquently clear that the White House expected every department of the Federal Government to cooperate with the National War Fund in every possible way; and third, because his appointment of Major General Philip B. Fleming as the Government liaison officer with the Fund gave the whole proceeding an expediter of the first order.

That prescription—involving the ingredients of top authority, instrumentality, and catalytic agent—will work as well as anyone can reasonably expect, always provided that it be remembered that authority in such matters is by consent rather than by police power, and that Washington always has a high degree of barometric sensitivity to pressures.

FAMILY RELATIONSHIPS

The family life of the National War Fund, like that of most community chests, was a little dash of Old Mother Hubbard, with a garnishing of the Old Woman Who Lived in a Shoe. But some days went by without even one crisis.

The principal difficulty, of course, was that there was never enough money to go around. Naturally, many of the agencies wished to supplement their programs in other ways, by running special campaigns for gifts-in-kind, by having certain gifts designated for extrabudget purposes, and here and there by seeking permission to solicit cash from nationality groups—on the plausible ground that such gifts would come freely if sought for a particular country, and would not be prejudicial to the success of local war funds.

Many years from now, it is possible that some of us may look back on all that as just so much good clean fun. At the moment, however, we still feel as though we had somehow managed to slip away from Custer's Last Stand.

Most of the agencies, to be sure, played the game fairly, and were good sports when the referee had to blow his whistle on an offside play. The management of the Fund, in turn, always tried to maintain a reasonable balance between the need for more relief and the need for maintaining in good order the state and local machinery to which all the agencies had to look for their major financing. We couldn't always be negative, but in the total interest of all the agencies we could never allow ourselves to forget that it is sheer folly to throw away dollars in order to pick up dimes.

This account, however, would be incomplete if we failed to note that there was some degree of chicanery, such as launching a supplementary effort first, and then seeking permission when it was too late to stop it—and sending checks back to donors, with the suggestion that they should purchase supplies for the agency, for the reason that cash had to be reported to the National War Fund, and would thus reduce the agency's net requirements. Any such tactics, obviously, kept the Fund itself in hot water with state and local war funds, and made for trouble all around—except, perhaps, in the mind of the agency itself.

Practically, the only solution for such a state of affairs is to make sure that all agencies are led and staffed by people who have integrity as well as skill, who put principle ahead of expediency, and who can see their particular cause in some fair relationship with all the other causes involved. No federation could afford to exercise its minimum controls by constant inspection, and no federation could live long on sheer authoritarianism or police power. Good will you must have, and good will was all that kept the agencies together in the National War Fund.

Finally, in this family account, there should be recorded a few major conclusions.

First, it should be said that the President's War Relief Control Board made a major contribution to agency management and control by insisting on certain minimum standards for agency registration, ultimately to the point of requiring that all members of governing boards should be American citizens, and that all programs be conducted "purely in the American interest." This tended to keep relief agencies out of factionalism, and to keep programs within the major aim of helping to win the war.

Second, there was no more important decision on the part of the Fund than the initial decision to avoid ex officio agency representation on the executive and budget committees. Members of these key committees of the Fund had a major interest in one or more of the agencies, to be sure; otherwise, many of them might not have had the motive to serve. But there was no official representation by agencies, and no one was expected to act on these committees as a special pleader.

Third, it is well to take a realistic view about the relationship of national agencies to any federated national appeal. Theoretically, each agency brings to the federation important resources in terms of fund-raising. Actually, most of them just go along for the ride.

In the case of the National War Fund, there were probably two reasons for this. Nationally, once an agency was freed from the fund-raising function, its leadership and staff tended to concentrate more and more on program, and less and less on finance—which is probably as it should have been. Locally, on the other hand, the constituency of the agency was often lost in the shuffle. It may or may not have been drawn into program operation, by serving in local workrooms or collecting gifts-in-kind, and was seldom integrated effectively in the local fund-raising operation, usually because local chests were already well organized, and often because no one seemed to know how to bring such integration about in any effective way.

Of one thing you can always be certain: that whenever there is or appears to be a conflict of interest between the national level and the local level, the local constituency of the national agency will always keep on the local side. Whatever the reasons, three national appeals for the USO and three for the National War Fund indicate clearly and conclusively, at least in the mind of this writer, that the agencies make the cause and the program, but never make the campaign.

COMMUNITY RELATIONSHIPS

A more interesting search for Diogenes, if he should ever come this way again, would be to look for the average American community. The dear old boy would end up, in our opinion, with sore feet and a sore heart.

The experience of the National War Fund turned up two basic conclusions in this connection; first, that this is a big country, and second, that communities vary just as people do—in the way they feel about themselves, and in their attitude toward others. The only way in which they are all alike, apparently, is the way they feel about someone coming in from out of town and telling them what to do.

As we pointed out in Chapter III, the best answer to the challenge of sheer geography is decentralization. The founding fathers really had something when they set up the states; only the states could have dealt with the community problems of the National War Fund. Let a local problem come up, and we at the national office promptly played ostrich. We would back up the states in any position they took, and would participate in any intrastate problem whenever a state asked us to do so, but that was all. Believe me, that was *all*.

But we were not oblivious, of course, to what went on in local communities. For that was where all the money was raised, and where the money had to start rolling on its way to the agencies. We watched, we listened, and we learned a few things.

The key to the character of any given community, in terms of federated fund-raising, is motive. It all depends on what the leaders of the community have in mind when they organize their local fund or chest.

If they have it most in mind to protect the contributors (among whom they themselves are probably to be numbered), then the resulting structure will be a sort of Chinese Wall—a defense mechanism in which success is measured by keeping budgets down and keeping new causes out. Such communities sometimes succeed, more often fail, and are strictly hardpan country for any national cause or agency. In time, of course, both the lay leadership and the professional staff become chronic pessimists and expert viewers-with-alarm.

On the other hand, if the leaders are interested primarily in health, welfare, and recreation, and really want to make the community a better place in which to live, then there is hardly a reasonable limit to what that community can do. They sometimes fail, more often succeed, and are the stuff out of which national causes grow and prosper. Short of accident, the lay leadership stays on a high level, and in the long run insists on competent and courageous professional staff. Both the leadership and the staff are constructive realists, always on the plus side, and ever all out for success.

Now it is customary almost to the point of dogma, we are aware, to lay all these variations at the feet of the long-suffering layman. The professional staff, according to the standard legend, has little or nothing to do with it; he merely executes the lay-conceived policy.

This, we submit, is the bunk, with no more validity than to claim that boards of trustees run colleges and hospitals, and that boards of elders and vestrymen run churches and parishes. And besides, the National War Fund lasted long enough to see what happened when communities changed their staff leadership, and what happened when staff changed communities.

The better the community, to be sure, the higher standard it will set for its staff, and the better staff it is likely to have. But in the long run, simply because it is the staff that does the full-time job, and because laymen must necessarily give such matters their secondary attention, it is our considered conviction that a local chest rises or falls with the caliber of its professional management. Put it high enough, and you have civic leadership as well as competent executive leadership for the chest. Put it low enough, and the chest's maximum life expectancy will be about three years. Put it in the middle, and you can go on forever—in the middle.

Nationally, except to pray that some day all big cities may be as well staffed as the best are today, there are only a few things you can do about these community variations. You can recognize that they exist, and leave them strictly to the states. You can avoid generalizations about "the chest movement," and thus keep out of fatuous foolishness. You can be friendly, but not partial. You can take a fair and consistent position, and stick to it, recognizing that a local concession today means a national retreat tomorrow.

Above all, you can arm yourself against the sorrows of the exceptions by reflecting that most people are really wonderful, and that you are probably getting all the breaks you actually deserve.

ORGANIZED LABOR

One of the brightest spots in the story of the National War Fund was the Fund's relationships with organized labor.

As explained earlier, both the A. F. of L. and the C.I.O. had planned relief campaigns of their own, which would have cut directly across the path of unity and federated fund-raising by soliciting gifts from union members, and also, in the case of the C.I.O., from firms and corporations with union contracts. The aim was in keeping with one of the oldest traditions of American labor. The plans had been carefully laid, after consideration and approval by the respective national labor bodies.

In 1942, at the request of community chests, and later at the request of the American Red Cross, both the A. F. of L. and the C. I. O. abandoned their plans for independent campaigns, and made common cause with the two annual major appeals—the Red Cross in the spring, and the chest campaigns in the fall.

That was the situation inherited by the National War Fund. The plan was reasonable, mutually agreeable, and highly productive. It democratized community campaigns by broadening the base of giving to a point never before achieved, and added many millions of dollars to war-time agency budgets, both for the war-related agencies and for homefront agencies for local health, welfare, and recreation.

Labor would have paid the costs of the two committees out of campaign receipts if labor had run its own campaigns. Otherwise, there was no provision in either organization for financing the work of such committees. That is why these costs were assumed by the American Red Cross and the chests, and later by the Red Cross and the National War Fund.

Why, it may be asked, was it necessary to organize and finance special committees for stimulating the participation of union members in community campaigns? Why with labor, any more than with any of the professions, or with management?

There were two reasons, and both good ones. For one thing, in prewar fund-raising there was tall talk about "broadening the base of giving," but with few exceptions not much was done about it. And it didn't matter much, as campaign goals were generally low enough so that success could be attained on the old patterns.

And then Hitler invaded Poland, with the eventual result that local goals were doubled and tripled, with income taxes shooting toward the stars. Employment and wages also shot up, so that the gold in them hills across the railroad tracks suddenly began to look like very fine gold indeed.

What community leaders thought about it was plain enough. But what was more important was what Tony and Pete and Mary thought about it, over in that shell-loading plant. They too were Americans, not only with friends and relatives in the armed forces, but often with close ties in the old countries. But they knew little or nothing about chests and chapters, and by all their traditions and experience were more likely to listen to the union steward than to the president of the First National Bank.

The point is that labor, previously on the outside and not even looking in, was now invited to a new kind of a party, the hosts of which were strangers, and traditionally antagonistic to labor unions. Put yourself in such a spot, and it won't take long to see that the task of swinging labor's rank and file into line, fast and in a big way, necessitated dynamic leadership and lots and lots of urging and explanation. That was the first reason why local chests and Red Cross chapters needed the field forces and publicity programs of the two labor committees.

The second reason has to do with campaign technique itself. Farms are scattered, so you call on farmers one at a time. Professional men and corporations have offices of their own, so you solicit them one at a time. Organized labor, on the other hand, with few exceptions, is found in groups—usually in large groups. So because calling on union members in their homes would cost more time and money, both for solicitation and the collection of pledges, you do the job where labor works, and you do it on a group basis. In principle, the problem is no different than selling group life insurance instead of individual policies. In practice, just as in the case of group life insurance, it calls for different planning and special techniques. So that is the other common-sense reason why there were labor committees, and none for farmers, professional men, and corporation executives. Labor had to help management work out the plans and techniques, and labor therefore had to send field people around to explain how to do it.

That is the essence of the story of the participation of the A. F. of L. and C.I.O. committees in the war-time task of the National War Fund and the American Red Cross, though much more could be said, and should be said elsewhere, about the by-products—the amazing increase in labor participation in health and welfare planning, and above all, the improved understanding and relationships between labor and management, simply as a result of putting a lot of feet under a common table for the united discussion of a noncontroversial cause.

Here was a truly great achievement, subject of course to the general trend of postwar recession and reaction, but one from which many gains are certain to be preserved, to the advantage of all and in the interest of unity and concord.

OTHER RELATIONSHIPS

For the rest of it, one is likely to fall into the ways of Gilbert's Sir Joseph Porter, K.C.B., who "polished up the handle of the big front door." The National War Fund got along nicely with everyone, thank you, and to tell all about it here might easily lead to just so much "apple polishing."

There are no lessons involved, except to remind ourselves again that most people are fair, decent, and friendly, and that the best way to develop sound relationships is to remember your ordinary good manners.

But we should record, nonetheless, that the National War Fund enjoyed happy and effective relationships with the American Red

Cross, the American Association of Broadcasters, newspaper and magazine publishers, the United Mine Workers, the Railroad Brotherhoods and other independent national unions, the War Activities Committee of the Motion-Picture Industry, chain-store associations, and closest of all, naturally, with Community Chests and Councils, Inc.

In fact, it is fitting to close this chapter by a special reference to the national body of chests and councils. It could easily take a personal tone, in an expression of genuine gratitude and lasting affection for Ralph H. Blanchard, the able and eloquent executive director, and the secretary of the National War Fund's board of directors. But we'll put it in broader terms.

The National War Fund lived by federation and succeeded by unity. Whatever its instinct may have been, it borrowed freely for policy, principle, personnel, and techniques from Community Chests and Councils, Inc., from the very beginning to the very end. It suggests now that it will be in that organization that the future will find the right seeds for the next great national experiment in joining all hands in some high and common cause.

VIII

WHEELS WITHIN WHEELS

From a business point of view, the task of the National War Fund was to translate an idea into a corporation with a sales volume of more than $100,000,000 a year, and then to translate the corporation into a memory—all within the space of a few years, and all at top speed.

We have recited how popular demand gave birth to the idea, how the corporation was organized, how the fund-raising operation was promoted and conducted, and what was accomplished with the total fruits of the effort. "The play's the thing," and that was the play.

The purpose of this chapter is to conduct a short tour behind the scenes, so that those who may be interested in the business phases of the Fund can see some of the essential facilities and procedures with which the Fund conducted its operations. This involves, we believe, a brief review of the plant and personnel at national headquarters, a glimpse of the problems of purchase and supply, and some little consideration of the baffling and complex question of quota systems.

· NATIONAL HEADQUARTERS

Originally, on the twelfth floor of the Empire State Building, the Fund had office space of some 8,700 square feet, which quickly proved to be inadequate. On May 21, 1943, therefore, the Fund moved to the Wadsworth Building, at 46 Cedar Street, where the peak amount of space, in December of 1944, was 14,976 square feet. At the end, toward the close of 1946, the space had been constricted to three small rooms. The important factor on space, we found, is to have enough but not too much; people work better when they are jammed up a little bit than when they are widely spaced out.

For reasons of economy, much of the furniture and equipment was borrowed, with each piece numbered and recorded to insure prompt return. Knowing at the outset that the Fund was to be a temporary organization, and faced as well by war-time shortages, other furniture and equipment was either rented or purchased secondhand. Happily,

101

when the time came for liquidation, the market for office equipment was such that all of the Fund's purchases could be resold at cost or better. It wasn't the sort of thing you see in the movies, but it worked, and in the end cost practically nothing.

The personnel problem was simplified by the fact that so much of the initial staff was merely transferred from the campaign department of the USO. At the peak, the clerical staff included extra typists and stenographers in accordance with the temporary requirements of the annual appeal, but the year-round clerical staff numbered only 43, with 18 secretaries, 5 typists, 7 clerks, and assorted specialists. Abnormal as the war-time conditions were, there was virtually no turnover. Employee practices probably had something to do with this, but the main reason was that everybody seemed to enjoy their work.

Headquarters services were kept under control by periodic staff meetings and by a consolidated daily report, which from the first recorded for each department all significant decisions and moves. That, together with written descriptions of the functions of every department, meant that every employee knew what he or she was supposed to do, to whom to report, and in general what was going on throughout the office.

As anyone could imagine, the national headquarters used the mail, the wires, and the telephones in a fairly big way. You can get some idea of the mailing problem from the fact that the Fund kept two girls busy cutting mimeograph stencils, and two more running the mimeograph and addressograph machines. In the three years the Fund used two million sheets of mimeograph paper, and nearly half a million ordinary envelopes. Telegrams averaged 300 a month, and at campaign time reached a monthly peak of 900. For telephoning, two operators worked a switchboard with 20 trunk lines and 60 office extensions, and handled a peak load of 6,000 calls a month. The daily average on long-distance calls ranged from a normal average of 20 to a peak average of 60 at campaign time.

All doors were kept open, no one was ever "in conference," and everybody played for the team.

PURCHASE AND SUPPLY

It took the Fund one whole dizzy year to learn that purchase and distribution should be centralized; not merely as a more efficient measure of budget control, but also in order to meet dates on deliveries.

After that initial year of letting each department requisition its own materials and arrange for shipments, the Fund engaged an experienced purchasing agent, who handled all requisitions, arranged for competitive bids by vendors, and followed all orders through for delivery on scheduled dates. Finally, he checked all bills against purchase orders, shipping orders, delivery receipts, and stock inventories.

The important element in the system was controlled decentralization. So far as possible, to save time and storage space, vendors were required to ship direct to state war funds, which in turn shipped to local communities. Only films and billboard posters were exempt from this general policy.

Scarcely less important was the fact that the distribution was kept within reasonable bounds by two general controls. The national office put a price, to be paid by the state war funds, on 22 items of campaign materials, the price covering mechanical production costs only. And when materials were issued to the states free, the national office set the quantities according to a materials quota system, state by state.

In 1945, the final campaign year, this centralized system of purchasing and distribution cleared a total of 71 items of campaign and publicity material, totaling 85,000,000 pieces. In that year, the budget for such materials was $430,200, the gross expenditures were $514,660, the income on purchases by state war funds was $146,129, and the net expenditure was $368,530—well within the budget.

THE QUOTA QUESTION

In any universal fund-raising appeal, to be carried to all the counties in all the states, half the money has to come from 6 states—New York, Pennsylvania, Illinois, California, Ohio, and Michigan. On the other hand, the 6 states at the other end of the list—North Dakota, Arizona, Vermont, New Mexico, Wyoming, and Nevada—will yield just about one and one-quarter per cent, or slightly less than you can count on from the single state of Tennessee.

How come, and who says so?

Well, it took a long time to find out, and our advice would be not to try to hold your breath under water until all 48 states are happily agreed on the subject.

It all started, innocently enough, back in 1940, when Community Chests and Councils, Inc., in cooperation with the United States Committee for the Care of European Children, sought to devise a method whereby some portion of the Committee's goal of $5,000,000 could be allocated to chest cities. The method decided upon, after much fine conversation had been tossed back and forth, was to use two simple factors: population, and known capacity for giving. This meant that local quotas were established at eight cents per capita of population in chest cities in which the per capita gift to chests had been less than $3.00 in the previous year, and ten cents wherever the chest per capita gift had been $3.00 or more. This was the first national quota system of World War II, and comparable in many respects to Henry Ford's first car. It was acceptable because it was simple and easy to understand, and because the goal was so modest that arguments were hardly worth while.

In 1941, when the USO put on its first campaign, for approximately $11,000,000, the 1940 quotas were simply doubled, and that was that. In this year, and in 1940, it should be noted, 65 per cent of the money was allocated to community chest cities, and the other 35 per cent was merely handed to New York City, with many a fine compliment, and the USO's warmest regards. (New York City was given a dollar goal, of course, with not too much talk about what it meant in terms of relative percentages.)

By 1942, however, the problem had put on its long pants. The USO wanted $32,000,000 this time, and it was all too clear that the other big cities could no longer work the 35 per cent shell game on their country cousins in Manhattan. At the level of $32,000,000, New York City simply could not raise that much money. So the decision was made to carry the appeal to all communities, including the 2,500 counties without community chests. The quota for New York City was reduced, the amount sought from chest cities was cut from 65 to 60 per cent, and the difference was allocated to the non-chest area on a straight per capita basis. This too worked satisfactorily, for that one year.

By the Fall of 1942, however, as recounted elsewhere, the war-related fund-raising situation was a monument of good intentions and wholesale confusion. It was at that point, with the National War Fund just around the corner, that Community Chests and Councils, Inc. made its own quota study, on the basis of economic and financial factors available for all of the 48 states. These factors were:

> 1940 Population (Urban plus 50% Rural)
> 1941 Total Income Tax Collections
> 1941 Individual Income Tax Collections
> 1941 Federal Employment Taxes

12/31/41 Bank Deposits (Excluding Deposits Between
    Banks)
1939 Wholesale Sales
1939 Retail Sales
1939 Wholesale Trade Employees
1939 Retail Trade Employees
1939 Wholesale Trade Payrolls
1939 Retail Trade Payrolls
1939 Industrial Payrolls
1940 Income Payments
1941 Cash Farm Income
1940 Motor Vehicle Registrations

The National War Fund, for its first appeal in 1943, was glad to take the community chest figures as one major factor, but felt that the current experience in giving should also be weighted heavily. It therefore took into account how much each state had contributed to the USO in 1942, and also determined for each state the relative purchase of "E" Bonds. The average for the three factors thus became the Fund's quotas for 1943.

For example, it was found that in July, August, and September of 1942, the state of Alabama bought .908 per cent of all the "E" Bonds sold nationally. Alabama contributed .847 per cent of the $33,000,000 raised in 1942 for the USO, and its relative percentage on the 15 economic factors studied by Community Chests and Councils, Inc. was .920. The average for these three percentages, .894, became Alabama's quota for the National War Fund, with figures for the other 47 states and the District of Columbia adding up to exactly 100, and with all quotas carried to three decimal points.

In practice, the 1943 campaign results ran close to the quotas, except in eight important states—Connecticut, Florida, Illinois, Massachusetts, New Jersey, New York, Ohio, and Pennsylvania. In these states, whether due to excessive quotas or inadequate campaign performance, it was apparent that the suggested shares of a fund of $125,000,000 were too high.

Yet it was also evident, after some inquiry, that the other 40 states could not take on the additional burden, and should not, therefore, be asked to raise more in 1944 than they raised in 1943. So that was one of the major reasons why the budget of the Fund was reduced for 1944 from $125,000,000 to $115,000,000.

At the same time, the 1943 experience had indicated one interesting and significant fact; namely, that most of the states in the Middle West, the West, and the South had reached or exceeded their goals. This, it was felt, might indicate that the center of giving in the United States was moving toward the Southwest, and that too big a load was being placed on the older industrial centers of the Northeast. Accordingly, the Fund's quota review committee, headed by J. Cameron Thomson, of Minnesota, decided in February of 1944 to reconsider the whole quota system, in light of the latest available data.

The committee took the most recent reports on the 15 economic factors of the old study by Community Chests and Councils, Inc., and took into account the 1943 quota and the 1943 results, limiting the 1943 results in any one state to 100 per cent of the quota in order to avoid inflicting a penalty for success.

The result of this reshuffle was that quotas were increased in 36 states and the District of Columbia, were reduced in 10 states, and stayed substantially the same in two states.

The results were better. All but five states reached their assigned quotas, and only one of these five failures could have been attributed to the quota itself. Accordingly, as a new study would have resulted in purely minor shifts, it was decided to let the 1944 quota system stand unchanged for 1945.

Only from one state was there any serious objection, and this was on the question as to whether the 1944 percentage should or should not be reduced by twelve-tenths of one per cent. The Fund said "no," as that would mean one or more other states would have to take up the slack. The state said "yes," and there the matter rested—amicably unresolved.

On any future occasion, of course, these state quotas would have to be restudied. And in that process, there are several points which in the experience of the National War Fund should be weighed with care:

1. Preferably, there should be only one quota system for all universal national appeals. The American Red Cross, to be sure, bases its quotas on chapters rather than states. But that difficulty is hardly insurmountable; all that has to be done is to add up the chapter quotas, state by state. The point is that whenever there are two or more quota systems, the door is open to argument and controversy, with the city or state concerned more than likely to advocate whichever figure is lower.

Ordinarily, of course, no one quota system can be fairly applied to all causes. The quota system of the National War Fund can be applied fairly to any cause with a universal appeal and with a high enough goal to justify the cost of universal organization. It could not be applied fairly to a cause with a limited constituency, or with a goal of much less than fifty million dollars.

When the point is made that there should be only one quota system, therefore, we mean that there should be one common system, rather than merely one common set of percentages. The system should include at least three sets of state percentages, for major, medium, and minor campaigns, depending on the probable scope of the causes concerned.

2. Quota systems, to gain maximum acceptance, should have widely representative sponsorship, especially from those states or regions which are likely to protest increases. The chairman of any such sponsoring committee should not be from New York City, and should represent a state in some position of accepted leadership.

3. All factors included in any universal quota system should be applicable with reasonably equal force to all states. One state, for example, cited as a reason for reducing its quota the fact that farm income had dropped 8 per cent in one year, not taking into account the collateral fact that if farm income were to be stressed as a significant factor, quotas in many other states would take a spectacular nosedive.

4. Again, care must be exercised to include as many common economic and financial factors as may be available. With only four or five such factors, almost anything can be proved. With fifteen or more factors, the law of averages works more fairly and is far more convincing to those asked to accept its verdict.

5. The authority for factors should be official. Population, for example, should be decided by the Census Bureau, rather than by the local chamber of commerce.

6. As stated in earlier pages, no national quota system should attempt to go beyond the state level. Nationally, using the same factors when available for all counties, it is helpful and desirable to suggest county quotas—but only to suggest. Local quotas should be decided by the several states, not merely because the states know the local variations better, but also because only the states can make local quotas stick.

7. Somewhere in every quota system, either nationally or on the

state level, there must be a factor of safety, or "cushion." To expect success in every state and every community is simply beyond the limits of human experience. Even one failure, therefore, by so much as a single dollar in a single town, will mean national failure unless there is a margin somewhere to balance such loss. One method to accomplish this, used in Michigan throughout the war, is to arrange in advance for sharing oversubscriptions as well as failures. A more dependable method, in view of the fact that too many local communities are likely to pay the net local quota and no more, is to see that each state adds to its net national quota a margin of not less than five per cent, as well as its state costs, before quotas are assigned to counties and local communities.

Nationally, the only place for such a factor, assuming that the budget has been prepared on the basis of rock-bottom need, is either in the contingency fund section of the budget, or else in the quotas to be assigned to our offshore territories. Whether any national cause could successfully follow local chest practice, by including a factor of some 5 per cent as a reserve against collections, is an experiment yet to be tried.

8. Finally, it should be emphasized that once a quota system has been agreed upon, no changes should ever be made in midstream. Annual changes can be made, and in normal times should be made, but never, never, never should any change be countenanced during the course of any one campaign. The other 47 states would doubtless be agreeable to any reductions in their quotas, under the Utopian circumstances that some one state should insist that its quota be increased. But not even the subtle influence of fissioned uranium could increase 47 state quotas after quotas have been assigned, just because one sister state wants its own quota reduced.

It takes more than a slide rule to establish a quota system that will really work well in practice. The ideal quota expert, indeed, would be a cross between Roger Babson, Jim Farley, and old Bill Klem; someone who knows statistics, knows people, and can "call 'em quick and walk away tough."

MISCELLANY

There were many other little cams and cogs in the wheels within wheels, but most of them were merely the usual routines of sound business practice: constant auditing, quarterly reviews of the administrative budget, proper certification for all expenditures, and the like.

The net of it was that the business side of the National War Fund, thanks to the vigilance and devotion of a great many people, was conducted with a degree of economy commensurate with its high purpose. (Percentagewise, as noted in the financial statement in Chapter V, the total of the Funds' own expenses—for administration, fund-raising, and publicity—was less than eight-tenths of one per cent.)

And then came the time for liquidation, just when the vast machine was functioning at its best. This, as we shall see, was no simple task—more difficult, in many respects, than the original task of building it up.

Uphill, it's an orderly and steady pull. Downhill, if you don't look out, the old wagon can get away from you.

I X

LIQUIDATION HAS ITS
PROBLEMS TOO

Harold Nicolson, in his recent book "The Congress of Vienna," states a principle that is just as true today as it was in the time of Metternich and Wellington. "Coalitions," he says, "begin to disintegrate from the moment that the common danger is removed."

Federations of voluntary agencies, like alliances among nations, are subject always to centrifugal forces which tend to tear them apart. Casting euphemisms aside, these forces are all forms of self-interest. And the same self-interest which impels organizations to get together in times of stress or emergency begins promptly to separate them as soon as the stress or emergency has passed.

Any form of effective cooperation, as we have observed, requires that some degree of self-interest must be sacrificed. And it appears to be one of the fixed patterns of human behavior that the sacrifice of self-interest must be paid its price.

There was sound Puritan morality in the union of the thirteen original colonies which grew to be these United States. Sacrifice for the good of others was much more than a merely moral or ethical aspiration; it was one of the rules by which the colonial fathers lived and died, and brought forth the new nation. But it was equally true that grave dangers pressed on the union for many long years, and may well have been the deciding factor which kept the centrifugal forces in check until the secession of 1861.

Let none of us be surprised, therefore, that V-J Day was the beginning of the end for the National War Fund. It had been put together in an hour of national peril, and as a measure of enlightened self-interest; on the part of Washington in order to fashion a better weapon for victory, on the part of local communities in order to conserve effort and cost, and on the part of the agencies in order to raise more money. It was held together by the strength and interplay of all these compulsions. But when the compulsions weakened with victory, disintegration followed as night follows day. The sacrifice of self-interest essential to effective cooperation no longer promised commensurate rewards.

That, we believe, is the philosophical interpretation of what happened after the Japanese surrender. It may be useful, however, to trace the actual cause of events, and to review the special problems which a period of liquidation seems to impose.

BEGINNING OF THE END

On Monday morning, August 6, 1945, the affairs of the National War Fund had settled down to the usual August routine. Budgets for the agencies had been established for a period of twelve months, ending September 30, 1946. State war funds had apportioned county and local quotas. Campaign publicity materials had been distributed many weeks before, and most of the local campaign organizations had enlisted committee leadership at every level. All that lay ahead was to establish standards of giving, by national solicitation of the usual list of key corporations and by advance gift solicitation locally, and to recruit and train the main body of volunteer workers. The period of question and uncertainty that followed V-E Day in May had passed. We were all settling down for "business as usual," with a good deal of talk about the possibility of an invasion of the main Japanese islands sometime in the fall. We certainly ought to finish the war, most people thought, within nine months or a year.

But that day came the first atomic bomb. Wednesday came the second, together with a declaration of war on Japan by Russia. Friday came the Japanese surrender offer, and on the following Tuesday, August 14th, came the unconditional capitulation. V-J Day, you will remember, was fixed by the ceremonies aboard the U.S.S. *Missouri* on September 2nd. But so far as the National War Fund was concerned, its middle name and its chief compulsion was gone on August 14th— just eight days after Hiroshima, and fully six weeks before the scheduled date for the opening of local campaigns.

You can guess what happened. The wires, the telephones, and the mails all carried the same story—questions about the plans of the Fund, and a general assumption that at the least the Fund would sharply reduce its budget and cut quotas accordingly.

It can be argued now, long afterward, that this was all illogical and unreasonable; that our armed forces could not be disbanded forthwith, and that the end of active hostilities meant little or nothing to the relief needs of the people in many lands. At the time, however, all of us were caught up in the vortex of an emotional storm in which logic and reason were impotent; a storm which all but grounded our air forces, beached most of our Navy, and critically weakened our position in Europe. Small wonder, then, that the National War Fund also got a little pushing around.

Whatever we were to do, it was plain, had to be done fast. Time was running out on campaign preparation, and yet no further campaign steps could be taken, either on advance solicitation or on the recruiting and training of volunteer workers, until it was clear what the National War Fund was going to do. And the intimation was clear and strong that whatever the Fund did, it had better be pretty good.

There was no chance to call a meeting of the executive committee, or of the budget committee, or of the agencies themselves. So we merely glued ourselves to the telephone, and talked to many people.

The USO, we found, had already consulted the Army and Navy, and was prepared to reduce its budget for fifteen months by $5,650,000. No other agency, however, felt that its budget should be cut; certainly, in light of the need, by no volition of its own. Almost all of the relief agencies were still facing the peak of the relief problem, and just beginning to find it possible, after V-E Day had opened the way, to do the full task to which they had set themselves.

Indeed, most of these agencies envisaged essential operations well into 1947 and beyond, which meant that they would need funds beyond September 30, 1946—the end of the period to be financed by the Fund in the appeal yet to be made, in the fall of 1945. In turn, this meant that all these continuing agencies would either have to rely on the National War Fund for these future operations, or would have to revert to independent appeals, beginning in October, 1946.

Local chests, on the other hand, anxious as they may have been to see quotas reduced, were still more anxious on another point. They agreed that it would hardly be feasible for the National "War" Fund to conduct another appeal in the Fall of 1946—fifteen months after the war had ended, and yet were as one voice in declaring that the last thing they wanted was to turn all these war-related agencies loose in October of 1946—just at the traditional time of community chest campaigns. They might or might not include some of these agencies as they had done in 1942, but they most certainly and emphatically and vehemently expected the National War Fund to straighten out that situation. Otherwise, they could not be held accountable for what might happen locally.

State leaders, knowing the local attitude, generally took the position that the quota question was less important than the question of how long the Fund expected to keep going. The quotas had been allocated and accepted, and most of the states felt they could maintain the quotas as they stood, provided they could announce that this was the Fund's final appeal.

Finally, we sought the verdict of some of the national corporations. What did they think about it, in light of the cancellation of orders for war materials, the outlook for reconversion, the obvious needs of the agencies, etc.? What they thought, we found, was that the current budget of the Fund was still defensible—if only on the general premise that we still had to win the peace, but that the situation in another year would be something else again.

The gist of all this, when reported by telephone to the members of the executive committee, was that we ought to make the coming appeal our last, and that budgets for the agencies should be stretched to fifteen months instead of twelve, which could be done by maintaining quotas for the previously established budget of $115,000,000 without too much agency hardship, in light of the voluntary budget reduction by the USO.

The decision to do just that was unanimous. It was explained to the agencies, announced to all state and local war funds, and interpreted in a number of supplementary ways—by a special leaflet, by speakers, by radio, by the press, and so on. To a degree anyone could reasonably have expected, the decision was accepted in good spirit by everyone. The questions had been answered, and leaders everywhere went forward with the final appeal.

Months later, in his annual report to the board of the National War Fund, at a meeting in New York City on February 4, 1946, President Aldrich, after tracing the vital accomplishments of the agencies, explained the decision to liquidate in terms which should have a meaning to all voluntary social programs:

And now, in face of what the National War Fund has been able to do, and in face of the continuing need, why is it that your Executive Committee decided after V-J Day that the National War Fund should conclude its appeal to the American people, with the view of liquidating by the end of 1946?

That was the decision, and I for one am now convinced more than ever that the decision was right, and that there is nothing in the decision that is inconsistent with our country's continuing responsibilities both to our own forces and to the distressed in other lands.

We were established as a temporary war-related organization, and if it is true that we do not yet have peace, it is equally true that we no longer have war.

We were also established to make a universal appeal for a unified budget, without regard to strength of constituency, community preference, or any other of the usual checks and balances which normally play a proper part in weighing the response of the American people to any given cause or project. This was both desirable and possible under war conditions. It may be argued that it is still desirable. But I do not believe there is any question that such procedure is now beyond the bounds of possibility. And the fact that the President's War Relief Control Board is going out of existence on March 31st is significant evidence, I think, that the public authorities share our view.

The problems we face are the new problems involved in establishing a world of peace. The new problems call for new measures, for new designs to fit the new circumstances. It is proper, then, for us to say that this particular instrumentality will soon complete the task for which it was fashioned, and should therefore step aside.

To be sure, we still have before us a number of important and difficult tasks . . . But the main part of the job is done, and I think there is a lesson in our decision for hundreds of private and voluntary agencies.

As an article of faith, all such agencies, in complete sincerity, will deny the suggestion that vested interest plays any part in their continuation, and rightfully insist that the existence of a need is reason enough that they should carry on.

The National War Fund is putting that question back to the people. In 1942, the people wanted the National War Fund, and they got it in February, 1943. In 1947, the people may want something comparable, for reasons that may be similar. Our view is that whatever the people want, they in good time will get, that the only healthy organism is one that comes up from the grass roots, and not down from an ivory tower, and that the only valid test for indispensability is an avowed readiness to step aside.

Antaeus, be it remembered, was strangled by Hercules because he failed to keep his feet on the ground. Organizations can die for the same reason; sometimes, unhappily, all too unaware that their day is done.

Let us, then, in good conscience, declare that we have done what we had to do as well as we knew how to do it, and that the time is not far off when we can say, as Simeon did, "Lord, now lettest thou thy servant depart in peace."

COLLATERAL PROBLEMS OF LIQUIDATION

Mr. Aldrich pointed out, you may have noticed, that we still had before us "a number of important and difficult tasks." And he never spoke a truer word.

Transition Problem. The decision to liquidate the Fund at the end of 1946 had the collateral effect of leaving two of the Fund's general partners in a deep, dark hole, threatening the cause of federation in its task of bridging the transition between war and peace.

Community Chests and Councils, Inc., which in normal times is responsible for the national promotion of community campaigns, is supported financially by grants from local chests, the grants being settled at the time when local chests usually determine their annual budgets in May, June, or July. The Fund's decision to make no appeal in 1946, coming late in August, caught the national chest organization, therefore, with a budget which had been adequate during the tenure of the Fund, but which was far from adequate if Community Chests and Councils, Inc. were to assume the promotional responsibility for 1946. And it was too late to go back to local chests for budget increases.

The Fund's Executive Committee, consistent with the policy of preserving federation's war-time gains, and in the belief that chests in 1946 would include many of the Fund's continuing agencies, decided that the Fund should help bridge this gap, and voted a subvention to Community Chests and Councils, Inc. in the amount of $121,770, to supplement the organization's 1946 budget, principally for campaign promotion. (Actual expenditure, $118,956.37.)

Organized labor's two national committees were left in a similar position. Their activities on behalf of 1946 campaigns were thought to be in the interest of the Fund's continuing agencies, as well as in the interest of federation generally. It was thought at the time, in the same spirit of optimism in which we believed many of the war-related agencies would be included in 1946 chest campaigns, that local chests would reassume the responsibility for financing the two committees, if some way could be found for covering the year 1946. The Fund's Executive Committee therefore voted a subvention of $200,000 to keep the two committees alive and active until an orderly transition could be effected. (The actual disbursements under this subvention were less than $145,000.)

To cover these and other expenses during 1946 and 1947, in light of the fact that there would be no new income after the final appeals in 1945, the Executive Committee set up a special fund for liquidation expense, out of which, as this is written, it seemed likely that all disbursements might total approximately $450,000.

Deferred Commitments. By the time of the final board meeting, on February 4, 1946, the states had reported a total of some $87,000,-

ooo, as having either been raised for the National War Fund or as having been pledged in the form of deferred commitments by local chests. In the latter category, it was reported, was more than a million dollars. The first task, therefore, was to determine the authenticity of the pledges, so that we could decide whether they could be counted upon safely in fixing the revised budgets of the agencies.

What had happened, you see, was that the quota problem had not been fully settled by the position the Fund had taken at V-J Day. We had told the chests that we would stretch agency budgets to fifteen months if the total budget could be held at $115,000,000, and that communities which accepted their full quotas for that amount would be protected against independent fund-raising by the Fund's agencies until the end of the fifteen months, or December 31, 1946. Any community which accepted less than its full responsibility, it was held, could be given only proportionate protection. We could not fairly insist that the full quota be raised, but we could insist, reasonably enough, that the community should make the full effort.

Most communities did accept the full quota, tried their hardest to raise the money, and that was that. A number of cities, however, arranged with the states to take some 80 per cent of the quota at that particular time, with the understanding that the other 20 per cent would either be included in the chest appeal in the following year, or else paid out of the chest surplus. In that way, they satisfied the requirement of full responsibility, and won immunity from independent agency campaigns until 1947. Some of these arrangements had been made orally, most of them in writing, and all, as far as we could determine, in good faith. The full list, in February, 1946, added up to something more than $1,200,000; deferred "commitments" by the responsible leaders of long-established community chests.

Well it was that we were somewhat conservative in counting on that money in making our own commitments to the Fund's agencies. For in the performance of the promise, 90 per cent of it faded away, on the ground that campaign conditions in 1946 were such that the chest "could not accommodate the deferred quota within any attainable goal," or when that wasn't true, simply on the ground that the chest was not convinced at that point that the National War Fund "really needed the money." In more than one city such positions were taken in face of the fact that the chest had accumulated substantial reserves during the years of the war-related appeals.

Three conclusions can be drawn from this and similar experiences.

One is that communities, like individuals, have distinctive characters of their own. The second is that the honorable performance of the great majority should not conceal the fact that there is always a fraction whose word cannot be trusted. And the third is that the difference between absolute integrity and apparent integrity reveals itself only in times of stress. (Incidentally, we concluded too that no one can rationalize faster than he who speaks in the name of Good Works.)

The lesson, if your cause is national rather than local, is that a bird in hand is worth far more than two in a bush, and that if you have to count on those two other birds, take a good long look at the bush.

Collection Problem. One of the major understandings, in connection with the Fund's decision to liquidate at the end of 1946, was that all the money raised and collected for the Fund should be transmitted to New York not later than September 30, 1946. By that time, at the latest, we had to know the exact figure on which we could pay off our agencies, if we were to bring our mutual affairs to a clean and orderly conclusion. This was explained ad infinitum, and nowhere met with objection.

But the great day came, and the amount still due the Fund was $7,145,000. We pleaded, we stormed, and we begged, with the result that four weeks later the amount still due was $4,984,000. We sent emissaries into the field, we wired, we wrote, we phoned. And on December 31, 1946, the day the Fund had expected to wind up its work, there was still to be collected more than a million dollars; despite the fact that we had been plugging away on the theme of prompt collections ever since V-J Day.

There were several reasons for this protracted difficulty in collecting the money people had contributed to the Fund back in the Fall of 1945.

As far as local chests are concerned, there were three reasons: one of habit, one of fear, and one of sheer cupidity.

Habitually, chests usually pay their local agencies in twelve equal monthly instalments. This is satisfactory to almost all agencies with ongoing programs, and is consistent with the usual chest practice of collecting campaign contributions in pledged instalments. In this particular year the reason had little validity, in light of the fact that most corporate gifts had been paid in immediate cash, and that pledges for most employee groups had been deliberately held to a short period because of the uncertainties of industrial employment. But habit is strong, and was certainly strong enough to keep many chests in the same old groove, despite the well-advertised plight of the National War Fund.

The second chest reason, the one of fear, was that so long as a chest still owed the Fund money, the chest retained some measure of police power. If any of the Fund's agencies broke the rules on immunity by conducting independent campaigns before 1947, the chest could crack down by withholding money. This doesn't sound very pretty, or as though some chests had a very high opinion of the integrity of the Fund or its agencies. But it was a factor in the collection problem, nonetheless.

The third reason, the one of sheer cupidity, was a minor reason, confined numerically to chests you could count on your fingers. We feel impelled to mention it only in order to point up one of the lessons of liquidation; namely, the necessity for leaving an open end on collections. The reasoning of these happily few communities was that if they stalled long enough, the Fund would liquidate and the money could then be retained for local purposes.

Finally, in addition to these three reasons in the local chest field, there was a general reason for collection delays—the sheer viscosity of deposited money. We've spoken of this before, and cite it here merely to complete the picture. Gordon S. Rentschler, our national treasurer, took it into account in his final general letter to the state treasurers, late in the Fall of 1946:

My suggestion, in connection with the audit in your state, is that you might go beyond the state books themselves, as Iowa has done, by asking each county or local treasurer to report that all county and local deposits have been forwarded, and the accounts closed. Recalling what happened after World War I, this will make sure that none of us leaves behind us any Rip Van Winkle deposits, which could come to light in later years, to our mutual discomfiture, as a reflection on the quality of our stewardship.

The lessons from this collection experience may be obvious. One is that the problem should be regarded from the outset as one of major proportions—a campaign in itself, to be planned, staffed, and operated with full realization that success comes hard. Another, less obvious, is that the collection process must be decentralized. The National War Fund would certainly have lost millions of dollars without the continuing interest and effort of its state treasurers. A third lesson, implicit in the total process, is that the only dependable understandings are those based on good will. Contract or no contract, the righteous will be righteous and the chiselers will chisel.

Budget Problem. What made the collection problem such a bed of sharp thorns was the multiplication of embarrassing difficulties for the agencies. The Fund could pay them no faster than money was received, obviously enough. But what was worse, as long as the Fund's accounts receivable were well in excess of the amounts still due the agencies, the Fund had to hold back some margin, in order to make sure it could deal fairly with all the agencies if the eventual collections should fall short of total budgets. Eventually, when it became apparent that we could not expect to collect all the money still due by the end of the year, and that some few chests were holding back in the hope that we would liquidate on schedule and leave their commitments untapped, we served general notice that the Fund would continue to operate until all accounts receivable had been collected. Accordingly, by arrangement with several major agencies continuing into 1947, we changed our schedule of payments to the agencies, so that we could pay them in 1947, on account of their 1946 commitments. This is what we referred to earlier in this chapter as "the necessity for leaving an open end on collections."

NUNC DIMITTIS

Now, of course, it can be told. By February 20, 1947, thanks to the unremitting vigilance of all the state treasurers, the long-term integrity of the average American community, and the savings that had been effected here and there in one or another of the agency budgets, the Fund had an apparent surplus of $1,200,000. This the Budget Committee, with the later approval of the Executive Committee, was happy to distribute to the agencies as a partial restoration of previous cuts in their allocations; with the understanding that any incidental future receipts would be distributed in the same relative proportions.

All that remained for the Fund to do thereafter was to await the reports of the agencies on what had been done with these final appropriations, to report in turn to the board, to chests, and to the appropriate authorities in Washington, and then to close the books, close the door, and call it a day.

After that, we could indeed pray, "Lord, now lettest thou thy servant depart in peace."

X

WHAT ARE WE GOING TO DO NOW?

Making a statue of Lady Bountiful, American model for 1947, would present the sculptor with a neat little problem. The trouble is that the good lady seems to have both feet firmly planted in the air.

Remembering what Hercules did to Antaeus, we ought to get those feet down to earth. And to do so, we must realize, involves a complex task of social engineering, in which many people and many forces would have to play a part.

From the implications of that task there is no escape, any more than we can get away from the kind of a world we live in. Our society is becoming more complex, and we are therefore more dependent on each other. It is also changing more swiftly, with the result that there is more social displacement. Rich or poor, we must climb the same hills and face mutual hazards; bound together indissolubly by the rope of common welfare.

This is coming to be understood, to a limited extent, by the constituencies of local community chests, which for roughly thirty years have been spreading the good doctrine that "charity" is an act of enlightened self-interest, that there is actual strength in unity, and that everybody benefits when everybody gives.

Generally, however, philanthropy is a force that seems to be running wild, like an engine without a flywheel, in a car without a steering rod—heading feebly for God knows where. And it won't do, we submit, to say that this is just one of the things that has to happen in a free and democratic country. Too many people can be hurt. Futility, frustration, and disunity are evil rains that can fall on the just as well as the unjust. Chaos can too easily become epidemic. And in an epidemic no one can be safe.

These things are believed to be self-evident: (1) that there is a great and growing need for the fruits of American generosity—in education, public health, social welfare, and relief; (2) that these needs are global as well as national and local; (3) that public and private instrumentalities each have a part to play, and that even together they can hope to solve only a part of the total problem; (4) that some reasonable measure of unity and harmony is essential to effective progress; and (5) that we are not likely to get very far, the way things are going now.

So let's look around and see what's going on. And then let's see whether what we now know can lead toward greater order and effectiveness.

CURRENT HIGHLIGHTS

Certain of the foreign relief agencies, formerly financed by the National War Fund, are again engaged in a competitive scramble toward goals which in the aggregate involve sure disappointment. Ten causes with total budgets of $28,804,705, for the last 15 months of the National War Fund, went before the National Budget Committee of Community Chests and Councils, Inc., with budgets for the 12 months of 1947 in the total amount of $41,091,575. Only three of these causes were seeking any less than they had been allocated by the National War Fund, and three others were seeking two to three times as much. All could justify the need, but only a few had a reasonable plan for raising the money. Inevitably, the average result will be a low return at a high cost. Worst of all, the result may be interpreted, plausibly enough, as one more evidence that a callous and weary America is becoming indifferent to the global distress of humanity.

National health agencies, through the rejuvenated National Health Council, have been trying to get together on some basis of balance and reason, in order to tackle the ills that assail the human body with some relationship to their frequency and importance. But they find the way blocked, in large measure, by the disproportionate success of two or three agencies, whose sure-fire emotional appeals seem to be too good a thing to give up. The result is as though we were lavishing millions on hangnails, and tossing mere pennies at the blights that kill us.

National agencies in the fields of character-building and recreation, unless they are buttressed by substantial operating income, still find themselves in the perennial position of meeting local resistance to national programs, principally for a reason all too common to most national agencies—failure to link national and local programs in a community of interest, and thereby to deal with program as an integrated whole.

Schools, colleges, and universities, under the double pressure of mounting costs and diminished yields on endowment, are again appealing to their alumni, generally about matters concerning which the alumni have not been kept informed. Three academic bugaboos beset such efforts: first, the traditional attitude that increases in tuition fees would threaten the democratic character of the student body; second, the fear that a capital campaign might blow a fuse by crossing wires with the annual giving of the Alumni Fund; and third, the apparent belief that all you have to do in a capital campaign is declare the need, organize, and solicit. (Some college of agriculture ought to pass the word around that harvest time must be preceded by (1) preparing the soil, (2) planting the seed, and (3) cultivating the planted ground until Nature has taken its course.)

At the same time, hospitals, museums, organizations of veterans, and countless other causes are also standing at the bar of American philanthropy, pleading their cases too for maintenance funds, construction funds, endowments, and bequests. Many are successful, but hundreds are barely holding on, seldom failing badly enough to go out of existence—as they would have to do in the competitive field of business—but seldom doing well enough to operate with any significant measure of influence and success. If you want to see some of these Kilkenny cats of American philanthropy, just analyze your own mail, or look in the telephone book sometime, under "Society," "Committee," and "League."

The result of all this will be positive, in the sense that many millions of dollars will be raised for many sound causes, and that many weak causes will be hastened toward merited liquidation. But the result may be negative in two serious ways: first, that many a good cause will not gain the support it deserves; and second, that many volunteer workers and contributors, overwhelmed by the sheer mass of appeals, may stage a spontaneous revolt against the whole field. Indeed, these negative results are showing up now; not only in the spectacular failure of many current appeals, but in the growing movement to set up state and local "screening" bodies for determining what causes should be permitted to seek funds, and for what amounts.

BRIGHT SPOTS

There are, of course, certain bright rays of light. The better foundations do what they can to bring about some order and sanity amid all this welter of worthy aspirations. The Negro colleges have taken a big step forward, thanks to the unselfish cooperation of two or three colleges with the strongest individual appeals, in their successful promotion of the United Negro College Fund. The United Jewish Appeal, with a constituency of not more than four million people, asked for $100,000,000 in 1946, actually raised $105,000,000, and then decided on a goal of $170,000,000 for 1947. The American Red Cross is consistently successful, boldly reaching high goals in the face of accumulated surpluses, for purposes most people only vaguely comprehend.

Community Chests and Councils, Inc. has made a move forward on voluntary national budgeting, and there is promise of more reason and understanding in the development of the National Social Work Assembly. There is also promise of greater order, among international causes, in the Advisory Committee on Voluntary Foreign Aid (Washington successor to the President's War Relief Control Board), and in the American Council of Voluntary Agencies for Foreign Service, Inc. —in which 58 organizations aim "to provide a means for consultation, coordination and planning so that relief and reconstruction programs abroad may be carried on in the most effective way."

Certain big corporations, it should be noted, have appointed board committees, as an established business routine, to consider and recommend ways in which their companies should support philanthropic causes; aided in doing so, incidentally, by the significant studies of the National Industrial Conference Board. And finally, for those who are interested enough to find out more about the causes to which they are asked to contribute, there is always the National Information Bureau, and locally, the Better Business Bureau or the community chest.

Perhaps you can point out similar rays of light, to indicate that the dawn may be breaking on a bright new day. In our view, however, the exceptions merely accentuate the general problem. What could be a mighty and purposeful force is still a feeble and aimless trickle. Let's try to find the reason for it.

CAUSE AND EFFECT

Our thesis is that the two major causes for this general state of affairs are a lack of understanding and a lack of spiritual motivation.

The misunderstanding begins with the very words we use. When we speak of "charity," most of us are not thinking of it in the Biblical sense, as an inherent attitude of compassion, but rather in the "Lady Bountiful" sense, as a transitory act of passing out sweets and goodies to the dear, deserving poor. Comfortable in our own security, but vaguely uneasy and disturbed by the momentary intrusion of problems we would rather not face, we react much as the pagans did; we propitiate the gods with a modest offering, and smugly go our way. Perhaps you don't like that. But let's be honest with ourselves. Isn't that just about it?

Intelligent giving, on the other hand, is based on a wholly different concept; an attitude that a request to contribute to a good cause is an opportunity to share proportionately in the challenging task of improving the common welfare. By this concept, giving is an act of constructive self-interest—an investment rather than a gesture, and therefore subject to thoughtful reasoning as well as to warmhearted impulse. You don't have to be Mr. Rockefeller to regard your giving in that light. Proportionately, remember, you can look at it as he does. And there's a staggering thrill in contemplating the kind of a world we'd be living in if everyone did just that.

Because this difference between thoughtless "charity" and constructive philanthropy is not sufficiently understood, it follows that we also fail to understand the basic purposes of our voluntary agencies and institutions, their true relationship to us and our own welfare, and the character of the responsibility to be shared if they are to do well what we ourselves would have them do.

But understanding alone is not enough. There must also be stronger spiritual motivation.

What happens when the spirit moves strongly is evident in a number of directions.

Charity, in a Biblical sense, seems to be a way of life with those whose faith is derived from the Law and the Prophets: the Society of Friends, the Jews, the Seventh-Day Adventists, the Church of Latter Day Saints, and other groups kindred to the fathers of the Colony of Massachusetts and the Rhode Island Plantations.

To a Friend, having "a concern" can take him around the world on a simple mission of neighborliness. The Jews and the Seventh-Day Adventists, impelled by Mosaic law, give out of all proportion to their numbers, to all good causes as well as to their own. And as for the Mormons, the old story of nineteenth century polygamy has blinded most of us to the fact that every good Mormon "tithes"—gives ten per cent of his income to the Church, as well as his other giving to secular causes, and also gives one whole year of his life, at his own expense, in selfless service to others.

With 24,000,000 Roman Catholics, comprising our largest single denomination, constant giving goes far beyond the giving of dollars. They have also given 186,000 of their sons and daughters to lives of complete and final consecration; 39,000 priests, 7,000 lay brothers, and 140,000 sisters. With all these, and with those who give freely of their time to the Ladies of Charity, and to the Society of St. Vincent de Paul, this Church can indeed call itself "Mother of Charities," both here at home and around the world.

The Protestant picture generally is too diffuse for accurate measurement or appraisal. There is evidence, however, that all Protestant denominations are awakening to the opportunities for global service. Those comprised in the Federal Council of Churches of Christ in America are setting out, for example, on a five-year goal of $130,000,000 to $140,000,000 for service to those in other lands.

We seem to have here both an old and well-established pattern and a new and significant stirring among the forces of Christianity.

In the old pattern there is an element of joining hands with God in thoughts about humanity, a dynamic attitude about the brotherhood of man, an active prompting of the spirit toward simple deeds that speak louder than lofty but passive words.

In the new developments there may be some recognition that the Christian church as a whole has lost something along the way, which must now be regained.

Perhaps Protestants have spent too much time and thought on differences in form and ritual, and too little on the fundamentals held in common. Perhaps all of us, in our spiritual lives, have slipped into the easy attitude that religion is nothing but standing to praise, kneeling to pray, and sitting to listen. Perhaps it's high time we became less self-conscious about the dynamics of religion and gave them a chance to work, not merely on the concerns of organized religion itself, but on all matters involving the common welfare.

And now let's review some of the major effects of all this misunderstanding and spiritual inadequacy.

Most important, in all probability, is the effect on leadership. The net of it is that there is not enough of it, and that too much of what we have is not what it should be. Too many consider board membership an honor rather than a responsibility. Too many have to be begged to lead, instead of feeling that they are being given an opportunity to render useful service. Too many want to "lend their names," instead of lending their talent and their time. Professionally too, because either understanding or the prompting of the spirit has come too late, there are not enough competent men and women to go around. All of which, as you can easily find, leads to vested interest and mediocrity.

It naturally follows, largely as a result of the inadequate supply of competent lay and professional leadership, that the techniques of philanthropy are still in the horse and buggy stage. There is too little social engineering, and too much passing of the tin cup. The best of the professional fund-raising firms, to be sure, have blazed many a new trail, as have the best of the local community chests. But the better the man in that field, the quicker he will be to admit that the art of raising money, in proportionate amounts and at a fair cost, is still in short pants—if not in still more rudimentary raiment.

Again it follows that the volume of our giving is generally low. It may sound impressive when you add it up in one bold guess at the national total, but the real story is to be found in the income tax figures. A beneficent law allows us, as individuals, to deduct contributions to an almost limitless variety of causes, up to within 15 per cent of our net taxable income.

An increasing number of alert and generous individuals are now doing what the law both allows and encourages, by annually putting aside 15 per cent of their income into irrevocable trust funds for charitable purposes—from which contributions can be made in larger or lesser amounts from time to time, according to need and desire, and regardless of any particular calendar year. Such funds, in effect, are individual foundations, enabling the donor to carry out a balanced and intelligent philanthropic program, with Uncle Sam paying a substantial share of the cost, even for those in lower income tax brackets.

But such persons are still the exceptions. By our own testimony— and certainly we are not giving ourselves the worst of it in making out our income tax returns—we are actually giving about two per cent. Obviously, a lot more bread could be cast on these waters, within the law and without hurting ourselves. But most of us are throwing crumbs, and the reason again is lack of understanding and all the other effects that follow.

So we go on assuming that such and such a cause must be all right because of the fine names on the letterhead; we go on guessing we ought to give something because the person who asks us is someone we know; and we go on writing checks for some standard figure we privately determine for ourselves—not so small as to make us look like a piker, and not so big as to make us look like a sucker. We're pleased, more or less, the cause has to appear to be pleased, but there isn't much about it to make the angels smile.

The total result, finally, is duplication, overlapping, frustration, wasted effort, and high cost. And is that good?

WHAT WE HAVE LEARNED

Now there isn't much point to all this painful recital unless we can determine ways to do something about it. So let's look now at some of the lessons learned in these past thirty years or so, many of which have been confirmed or sharpened up during the major and nationwide experiences of the National War Fund.

These are things, we believe, that have been attested on a broad enough scale, and over a long enough period of time, to acquire the validity of fundamentals:

About the United States. First of all, we have learned to beware of easy generalizations about this great country of ours. When it comes to customs and points of view, from Maine to California is farther than you think; what may look like fine spinach in Minnesota may seem at the Gulf of Mexico to be just so much poison ivy. The states know these differences much better than you can possibly know them, sitting there in your national Ivory Tower. So the first lesson is to keep your national pattern clear and simple, and to decentralize as fast and far as you can.

About People. Geography and local differences aren't the only factors which call for decentralization. People aren't just statistics at the Census Bureau; people all live somewhere, and where they live is where their hearts are, and where their thinking starts. So the lesson is that you don't talk nationally—you talk locally.

We learned too, as others have, that habit is a powerful force but hard to establish; that people tend to go for easy and symmetrical patterns, and have to be led to proportionate giving; that people generally prefer to see the good they can do rather than the evil they can undo; that people tend (1) to do what other people do, (2) to repeat pleasurable experiences, and (3) to be responsive, but not analytical. We have learned that the people in any given community have a measurable attention period, beyond which you can't keep them interested. We found too that most people are very fine people indeed, and that the few exceptions were just born that way, and you can't do anything about it.

Most important of all, as the American Red Cross learned many years ago, we found that loyalty is born of interest, and that interest is the child of participation. As long as people work for a cause, and weave something of themselves into the moving fabric, that cause has powerful and lasting friends.

About Organization. No organization, we found, is ever stronger than its leadership, or ever reaches farther than the degree to which the leadership group is representative of the groups from which support is to be sought.

Those twin principles are the rocks on which organization either builds or founders. But we have learned too, as others doubtless have, that national organization is a two-way process, like an accordion, rather than a one-way-at-a-time process, like a sliding trombone. What reaches out nationally has to meet something coming up from the grassroots.

Our old friend "decentralization" comes in here too. Nationally, you must work by authoritative advice rather than authoritarian control. Locally, to organize volunteers effectively, good organization means breaking big jobs down into little jobs, by the planned distribution of assimilable work units.

Organization grows best by personal contact, and keeps its quality, both on recruiting and solicitation, only by establishing the contact on an equal or higher level.

Finally, we know that an organization is no more than lines on a chart unless there is wholehearted indoctrination and infectious enthusiasm. This is a matter of well-planned meetings, dramatization, participation, recognition, the light touch, and a general atmosphere that every participant is a great man, and that this is the best of all possible causes.

About Publicity. Function, it has been reaffirmed, is always more important than machinery; the case to be made for a cause, therefore, should always be bigger than the cause itself. Agencies and other instrumentalities are only a means toward an end, and in themselves are seldom a matter of public interest or concern.

Next in importance, in the field of publicity, is the finding that the strength of an appeal is directly proportionate to its personal application. "Your Red Cross is at his side" was a war-time slogan that hit this particular nail right where nails wear their hats. And we also like to cite the slogan used in Dayton back in 1913, after a receding flood that drove people to the tops of their houses—"Remember what you promised when you were up in the attic."

Publicity, we found again, needs sincerity, simplicity, dramatization, repetition, and universal identification. For maximum visibility, as well as for reasons of economy, its distribution should be decentralized. For maximum acceptance, the atmosphere should be one of full disclosure, so that everyone will know that you are ready to tell all. But as all most people really want to know is just enough to rationalize their impulses, the secret of it is to show the full menu, but to point out the roast beef.

Finally, let publicity play its natural role, as information, reminder, and sound effects. Don't expect that publicity in itself will raise money. You can't stage an opera without music, but neither will the opera get very far unless somebody gets out on the stage and does something.

About Raising Money. If you are likely to forget everything else, just remember that there is really no such thing as a "national campaign"; funds must always be raised locally. Nationally, you can plant the seed, cultivate the soil, trim and spray the tree, and see that the fruit is gathered promptly and fairly distributed. But the tree has to grow in Brooklyn.

In that one fundamental are to be found several significant corollaries. First, any national cause should have democratic and proportionate representation. Second, the program should reflect local as well as national planning, in order to achieve maximum universality of endorsement and advocacy. And third, just as the strength of any individual appeal is directly proportionate to its personal application, the strength of any national appeal is directly proportionate to the strength of its roots in local communities.

The strongest roots, with the greatest national nourishment, are those based on active participation in program, like the local chapter workrooms of the American Red Cross. Add a planned local budget to the national budget, as the Red Cross does, and you have an unbeatable combination. Purely arbitrary budget divisions between national and local, such as 50-50 plans, are indefensible from the point of view of sound social planning, but are undoubtedly effective in raising money.

There is a lesson here in the final appeal of the USO. It was unsuccessful in raising only $19,000,000 for the last year of its operations, despite approval by returned veterans, urgent backing by the Army and Navy, and the obvious need for sustaining morale among 200,000 still in hospitals and some 1,500,000 relative youngsters still in active service. It isn't enough to say that the reason for the letdown was that the war was over, for the war was also over for the American Red Cross, in the spring of 1946. The main difference, in our opinion, was that as the USO reduced its budget, it reduced local domestic operations, and as volunteer participation was brought to a halt locally, public interest dropped off; with the result that the USO became a strong cause with a weak constituency—a fine tree with weak roots.

A few more lessons are worthy of brief reminders: giving must be proportionate, quotas must be worked out at every level—from each state down to each individual giver—operations must be decentralized, and allowance must be made somewhere for the inevitability of local failure here or there.

You might remember too that the philanthropic center of the United States—in terms of capacity for giving—is moving toward the Southwest. (Los Angeles was the only major city in the United States to raise its full quota in the last appeal of the National War Fund.)

Finally, you will do well to bear in mind that fund-raising is always subject to a law of diminishing returns; the wider the periphery, the greater the effort and the greater the cost. Only causes with a universal appeal, and with a universal constituency, can afford to seek universal support.

About Federation. Nationally, successful federation must lead from strength, not from weakness. The more important the cause, therefore, the more difficult it is to set it up, by finding compulsions that are strong enough to bring about unity in the face of reluctant and centrifugal forces of conflicting self-interests. You might say, with some reason, that the consummation of a strong national federation has many of the elements of a shotgun wedding. Certainly you can conclude that any national federation is bound to fail if it is nothing more than a mere huddling together of otherwise weak and impotent forces.

It follows, as we have stressed elsewhere, that successful federation, like any form of effective cooperation, requires some sacrifice of self-interest; that it must fairly represent all the parties concerned; that it must hold the sole franchise for raising money for the agencies involved; that its budget must be proportionate and realistic; that its constituent agencies must espouse comparable causes, with some reasonable common denominator in terms of public appeal; that the financing should be for net requirements only; that quotas must be maintained for the budget as a whole, even though individual donors be allowed to designate their gifts to one or more particular agencies;

and that budgeting should be frequent and flexible, without interference in actual agency programs.

Many believe that the National War Fund also proved that national
federation can be an effective force, better for all concerned. Never,
certainly, had so many given so much to achieve so wide an aim. Many
think that the Fund proved too that voluntary agencies can work effectively with public agencies, and that public agency participation, indeed, is essential to national federation.

Many local chests now believe there is nothing to fear in the concept of a national chest, and some wish there were one. But local chests
and national agencies too are still somewhat in the position of the
little girl who wrote this Christmas thank-you note: "Dear Grandma:
I have always wanted a pincushion—but not very much."

About Procedure. To keep things going as smoothly as possible, in
a world so full of imperfection, we would suggest that every public
cause take a few trial steps before it starts the race toward its goal. First,
define your purpose or objective in specific terms. Second, collect all
the pertinent data—facts and opinion—on the broadest possible front,
to obtain the widest possible representation and participation. Third,
weigh these findings in terms of comparable experience and accepted
standards. And fourth, plan what you are going to do in the light of
six basic questions:

1. *Leadership*—how much is needed, and where is it coming from?

2. *Support*—how many gifts, and gifts in what amounts, are needed
in order to make the quota, and where are these gifts coming from?

3. *Workers*—how many workers are needed in order to see all pros-
pects personally, where are the workers to be obtained, and how are
they to be recruited and trained?

4. *Publicity*—what needs to be said, and how is it going to be told?

5. *Timing*—what are to be the principal campaign steps and events,
and how are they to be timed?

6. *Cost*—how much is it going to cost to set up and operate the
necessary organization and publicity, and where is the financing coming from?

After that, go ahead and operate, if all the questions have had good
answers. But we would add this advice, from the experience of the
National War Fund—always keep good records, and remember that
to do so means a constant struggle. Some people like to recite, and
many like to remonstrate; but we never found anyone who liked to
report.

Finally, on this matter of procedure, it should be emphasized again that a good campaign, in every respect, is essentially a public relations operation; an art rather than a science, and a human experience rather than a mere interplay of techniques. Certain it is that he who would seek to understand the ways of raising money must first seek to know the ways of his fellow man.

Principal Conclusions. To help us remember something from all this, what five lessons are probably the most important?

For our part, we would suggest (1) the importance of careful *planning*, (2) the fact that the quality of the lay and professional *leadership* is the greatest single determinant of success or failure, (3) the importance of *decentralization* in the framing of program, the shaping of the organization, the promotion of interest, and the solicitation of support, (4) the necessity for *participation* in order to promote interest and sustain loyal advocacy, and (5) the principle that all *giving should be proportionate*.

POSSIBLE FUTURE STEPS

And now, with these findings before us, what are some of the steps that might be taken in order to make our giving more effective? What might be done to bring about better understanding and stronger spiritual motivation?

To write a program for the future of American philanthropy is beyond the purpose of this particular chronicle, and beyond the capacity of any one man, or any small group. We do believe, however, that any thoughtful person, merely on the premises advanced in these few pages, would reach a number of tentative conclusions.

So let's explore some of the possibilities together, as a sketchy process of sheer speculation on what might be done, in one field after another:

Schools and Colleges. Privately endowed schools, colleges, and universities depend for their very existence upon a continuing understanding of the role and problems of voluntary institutions. The way things stand today, they can no longer count on the large-scale beneficence of a few rich men; they must perforce broaden the base of their support, and raise the general standard of alumni giving.

Why, then, is it not in order to indoctrinate their alumni while they still are students? Why not introduce into curricula something about community organization, something about our voluntary institutions, something about the practical aspects of *noblesse oblige?* If orientation courses are good for freshmen, to show what college offers them, why not orientation courses for those who are about to graduate, to show them what there is in life besides earning a living and raising a family?

It is a commonplace, to the point of tiresome banality, that these institutions talk of "training leaders." Why not train a few? Why not explain to youth what leaders do, what their responsibilities will be, what trusteeship involves, and how voluntary leadership, when really effective, can help them and help others too?

Incidentally, universities have a chance to raise the whole level of voluntary effort by offering professional training for those who might dedicate their careers to administrative work in the fields of health, welfare, recreation, and education. There is one such school at Ohio State University for community chest executives. If there were others, the level of effective operation among all voluntary agencies would rise sharply in less than ten years. And many able young men and women would find a happy and exciting life.

Foundations. Generally speaking, foundations seek to demonstrate, but not to lead; to explore, but not to settle down. As the pioneer force in philanthropy, they thrust out at the frontiers of human knowledge and behavior, and are ever so careful not to be put in the position of appearing to dictate institutional policy or program. And with none of this could any reasonable person disagree.

But it is also true that foundations must hope that others will come along on the trails that have been blazed, and must be disappointed when others fail to follow. They must know too that the usual reasons for such failure are lack of understanding and institutional ineptitude.

Some foundation, then, may find it worthwhile to spread a little more understanding, and perhaps to explore further the ways in which institutions can more effectively help themselves.

Churches. Despite the fact that every church seems to be constantly immersed in problems of public support and finance, we know of no seminary that gives its students even the most rudimentary glimpse of community organization and voluntary finance. The deans always say the curricula are already overburdened with the older courses. The chance some church has here speaks for itself, in loud and eloquent terms.

But surely time can be found in Sunday schools to teach "earn, give and save," as the Y.M.C.A. and the Boy Scouts do, for instance. Surely all the churches, certainly the Christian churches, can better prepare their own growing constituencies on the sacrificial meaning of Brotherhood. And if they can't do anything else, they might just let it be known that the word for "charity" in rabbinic Hebrew is "zedakah," or righteousness.

National Agencies. It may seem like an oversimplification, but one of the best moves national agencies could make would be to stop calling themselves national agencies. As such, when they get to the local level they are apt to be just so many carpetbaggers.

The point here is that acceptance for national programs must come from the grass-roots, and must have unity all the way. This cannot be achieved so long as it appears that local program is one thing and national program another, or that part of the money can be raised locally and another part nationally.

The lesson, whatever the field, is that the so-called national cause has to take root in local communities, with local participation at every step of the way, and with local retention of funds raised in a common national cause based on advance budgeting only. This is the way of the tortoise, perhaps, but what we heard is that the tortoise is the one who won the race.

American Business. Individual corporations are coming more and more to regard giving to health, welfare, and recreation as part of the cost of doing business, on the ground that business prospers as communities prosper. Management, we predict, will arrange for standing board committees on these problems, will deal with them constructively in annual reports to stockholders, and will actively encourage fellow officers to take positions of leadership in voluntary community causes.

On the association level, however, the National Industrial Conference Board is the only body, so far as we know, that has taken a significant step toward accepting philanthropy as an integral part of the "free enterprise system."

The National Association of Manufacturers, for example, has yet to recognize that its members play a substantial part in the financing of health and welfare agencies, that much has to be done to set standards for evaluation and giving, to develop industrial case histories into common practices, and in general to interpret to business and to the public what American industry does for the common welfare.

The United States Chamber of Commerce might note the fact that local chambers of commerce are again bestirring themselves, as they did a generation ago, about the multiplicity of campaigns and the necessity for better screening of appeals. These moves, in Cleveland, Detroit, and elsewhere, may be considered negative, in that the motivation is defensive. But that is merely the natural result of the confused and competitive situation, and on the constructive side is significantly comparable to the chamber of commerce point of view after World War I, an important factor at that time in the growth of the community chest movement.

Sooner or later, we predict, these and other national associations in commerce, industry, and finance will make this whole subject part of the regular order of business, and thus help make for better understanding.

Incidentally, it will be found rather pleasant to discuss a subject so important and so universal, and yet so free from controversy. Moreover, it may be found that voluntary action is preferable to the involuntary philanthropy devised by John L. Lewis, whose royalty plan of five cents a ton, as this is written, had already amassed a health and welfare fund in the amount of $15,500,000.

Organized Labor. The war-time efforts of the American Federation of Labor, of the C.I.O., and of many independent unions, should certainly be extended and intensified, not along the separatist lines of the International Ladies Garment Workers Union, but along lines of community organization. Ways will surely be found to bring this about, so obviously is it in the interest of a unified America, as well as in the interest of organized labor itself.

Professional Groups. Voluntary agencies, if only because they are voluntary, run the constant risk of becoming too professionalized. And yet all such agencies need the most competent professional help they can get. Therein lies the perennial dilemma of the professional group; how to follow the subtle line between the leadership that should be the layman's, and the management that should be the staff's.

The professional will do well to seek always the first-class counsel of first-class laymen. For he must know that nothing he can do will ever lift a voluntary cause higher than the scope and quality of the effort of the volunteer.

The layman will do well to remember always that cheap help is expensive help, and that the best investment any agency can make, at almost any price, is an investment in top staff—people with integrity, stability, and common sense.

Information Channels. The press, the radio, and national magazines have a fearful responsibility for the common welfare, and on the whole discharge it remarkably well. What they could do if there were better general understanding is almost beyond speculation.

Meanwhile, the leaders might delegate one or more editors or reporting specialists to the task of acquiring authentic background for material on health, welfare, and recreation, just as they do now on aviation and other special subjects—and that will be good. It would also be good if all of our leading channels of information should do a little checking, before they go overboard on a cause, with the analyses of the National Information Bureau.

Community Chests. Nationally, the chest movement has a chance to extend national budgeting, and to help add a few more molars to the processes of the National Information Bureau. It can help national agencies in many ways other than steering them toward local chest inclusion, and will doubtless do so. Its opportunities are as broad as the field of human welfare, and it will move through that field as fast and as far as the grass roots will let it move.

The real questions are local questions: whether any given community prefers to live for itself alone, or whether it really wants to be part of the United States; whether the chest prefers to be solely the creature of certain member agencies, or whether it wishes to speak for the entire community on all matters relating to health, welfare, and recreation; whether its operations are to be restricted to the operations of the chest and its agencies, or whether it intends to open the door for aid and counsel, regardless of whether a cause is or is not included in the chest.

Here evolution is at work. Some chests are one way, some another, and some just in-between. As understanding comes, and as the level of competent leadership rises, the top achievement will be far beyond the heights we now see.

And then there's you and me. All of this, each can say to himself, depends on what others do. These things will come about as determined leaders stir themselves. Meanwhile, there isn't much for individuals to do.

One thing, however, each of us can do, and that is to seek better understanding, and then to set standards for ourselves in order to make our own participation more effective.

For one thing, when we agree to be a worker we can really work, and not merely lend the use of our name. This means giving study to the cause and time to the effort. It also means, as many can tell you, a degree of lasting satisfaction impossible to describe.

For another thing, we can give proportionately and with discrimination. We don't have to give just because we're asked to do so. In fact, in some cases giving can do the mischief of keeping alive a cause that has lived far beyond its day. But we should feel the compulsion of giving each cause a hearing, and then judging it by certain minimum standards.

"What is the basic problem with which this agency is concerned? What is this agency planning to do, in light of other attacks on the same problem? Is the plan timely and well conceived? Are the trustees competent and active? Does the staff know its business? Is the budget reasonable and what is it costing to raise the money? What are others giving? How much am I supposed to give? And is such a gift proportionate to my income and the gifts I make to other causes?"

These are not all the questions, but most of the time these are questions enough. Or you can, of course, ask your local chest executive, who has access to National Information Bureau reports, and who will know whether or not the cause has been reviewed by the National Budget Committee. You might also find it significant, many times, to ask the person who solicits you how much he himself gave.

Whatever the technique, the point is that all of us can bring about greater order and effectiveness by adding thought to impulse. By all means, let's give free rein to our generous emotions. But let's give our intelligence a chance too, by thinking before we act.

SO WHAT LIES AHEAD?

Eventually, perhaps, there may be a national chest, through the federation of enough strong agencies to cover all of the major fields of health, welfare, and recreation. Such a chest, through sound budgeting and universal promotion, could doubtless eliminate most of the current confusion, and bring about something like a balanced pattern in program—at a cost far less than the total cost of today.

More immediately, there is promise in the plans of the National Health Council, for federation only in the field of health agencies. There is strong resistance here, both among a few of the agencies and among certain local chests. But unity will come when the people want it; first, by a demonstration in one or two key states; second, by the spreading of current local revolt among businessmen against the cost, multiplicity, and confusion of the current chaos; and third, as understanding spreads, by a curtailment of indiscriminate giving on the part of the general public.

Meanwhile, existing machinery can be made to work more effectively.

Schools, colleges, and our national channels of public information can work for better understanding. Foundations, corporations, and national associations can help set higher standards. The National Budget Committee and the National Information Bureau can broaden and sharpen their accepted functions. Local chests can keep their leading contributors better posted on extra-chest causes. Local chambers of commerce can do more screening on approving new causes, and yet keep on the plus side by more strongly advocating leadership for causes that are really worthwhile. Organized labor can go far merely by holding to some of the basic patterns of unity so well established in war time. And the churches, with their established constituencies and their limitless power of spiritual motivation, can probably do the most of all.

The essence of it, as in all human affairs, lies in the happy juncture of leadership and public demand.

A pattern has been hammered out by the compulsions of war. What we ever make of it will depend on the depth of our desire and the force of our decision.

The signs, we think, will be a rising tide, and the news that "six men gathered around a table."

NOTES ON APPENDICES

Historically, the key documents of the National War Fund were: (1) the certificate of incorporation and bylaws, (2) the standard agreement between the Fund and its agencies, and (3) the standard agreement with the state war fund organizations.

The relative quotas assigned to the states have been shown in the table on page 64, accompanying the text. The general method employed in state organization is outlined here among the appendices.

Finally, the appendices include directories of the Fund and its standing committees, of the agencies, and of the constituent state organizations.

Appendix A

CERTIFICATE OF INCORPORATION *

OF

NATIONAL WAR FUND, INC.

Pursuant to the Membership Corporations Law

We, the undersigned, all being of full age and at least two-thirds of us being citizens of the United States, and at least one of us being a resident of the State of New York, desiring to form a corporation pursuant to the provisions of the Membership Corporations Law of the State of New York, hereby certify as follows:

First: The name of the proposed corporation shall be NATIONAL WAR FUND, INC.

Second: The purposes for which the corporation is to be formed are as follows:

To plan, promote, organize, manage, supervise, conduct and coordinate, directly or indirectly or in collaboration with other persons, the solicitation and raising of funds, by public appeal, public subscription or otherwise, for charitable, religious, literary, educational and scientific needs related to or arising out of war, including maintenance of the morale of members of armed forces and of civilians affected by war, and including relief of needs, material and spiritual, created by or arising out of war, its incidents and consequences.

To prepare and promulgate budgets, programs and plans for the above purposes, as well as policies and procedures, and means and methods, to be adopted for obtaining such funds; to allocate and distribute the task of raising funds for such purposes; and in that connection to collaborate with, and coordinate and participate in the activities of, relief associations, service organizations, war chests, community chests and other persons engaged in such activities;

To solicit and collect funds and contributions, and to receive by gift, deed, bequest or devise, and otherwise to acquire, money and property of every kind and description for the purposes herein described;

To hold, administer, allocate, distribute, expend, contribute, use and otherwise dispose of its funds and resources for any and all of the charitable, religious, literary, educational or scientific purposes hereinabove referred to, either directly or by allocating, distributing, expending, contributing or advancing the same to relief corporations, service organizations or other non-profit bodies, for use by them for any or all of such purposes.

* As filed in the office of the Secretary of State of the State of New York on January 12, 1943.
By-laws as amended to February 5, 1943.

140

In pursuance of and not in limitation of the general powers conferred by law and the objects and purposes herein set forth, it is expressly provided that the corporation shall also have the following powers:

To do all such acts as are necessary or convenient to aid the objects and purposes herein set forth to the same extent and as fully as any natural person could or might do, and as are not forbidden by law or by this certificate of incorporation or by the by-laws of the corporation.

As a non-profit corporation, none of the income of which shall accrue to any member, to purchase, receive by deed, gift, devise or bequest, hold, mortgage, lease, sell or otherwise acquire or dispose of such real or personal property as may be necessary for the purposes of the corporation.

To have all powers that may be conferred upon charitable corporations formed under the Membership Corporations Law of the State of New York.

Third: The territory in which the operations of the corporation are principally to be conducted is the United States of America.

Fourth: The principal office of the corporation will be located in the Borough of Manhattan, City, County and State of New York.

Fifth: The number of directors of the corporation will not be less than three nor more than one hundred.

Sixth: The names and places of residence of the persons to be the directors of the corporation until its first annual meeting are as follows:

Name	Residence
Winthrop W. Aldrich	15 East 78th Street, New York, N. Y.
Chester I. Barnard	333 Forest Road, South Orange, New Jersey.
Ralph Hayes	Hotel duPont, Wilmington, Delaware.
Gerard Swope	The Croft, Ossining, New York.
Henry M. Wriston	180 Hope Street, Providence, R. I.

Seventh: The corporation shall not have the power to conduct any activities set forth in subdivisions 1 or 2 of Section 11 of the Membership Corporations Law.

Eighth: Of the persons hereinabove named as directors, at least one is a citizen of the United States and a resident of the State of New York.

IN WITNESS WHEREOF, we have made, signed and acknowledged this certificate this 28th day of December, 1942.

WINTHROP W. ALDRICH
GERARD SWOPE
RALPH HAYES
HENRY M. WRISTON
CHESTER I. BARNARD

BY-LAWS

OF

NATIONAL WAR FUND, INC.

Article I. Purposes of the Corporation.

Section 1. The purposes for which this Corporation is formed are those set out in its Certificate of Incorporation. It is not organized for pecuniary profit and no part of the net earnings of the Corporation shall inure to the benefit of any private member or individual and no part of its activities shall be the carrying on of propaganda or otherwise attempting to influence legislation.

Section 2. As provided in its Certificate of Incorporation, the Corporation may, in carrying out its purposes, allocate, distribute, expend, contribute or advance its funds and resources to relief corporations, service organizations or other non-profit bodies. The Board of Directors, or the Executive Committee or any special Committee or Committees thereunto duly authorized, shall have power to determine the eligibility of such corporations, organizations or bodies for such purposes, and to determine the allocation, distribution, expenditure, contribution or advance of funds and resources of the Corporation among them, to determine the time or times at which, and the territory or territories in which, the Corporation's campaign or campaigns for funds shall be conducted, to fix the amount or amounts to be sought in such campaign or campaigns, and to determine and allocate quotas in such campaigns among the respective territories concerned.

Article II. Offices of the Corporation.

Section 1. The main office and place of business of the Corporation shall be in the Borough of Manhattan, of the City of New York.

The Board of Directors or Executive Committee may establish other offices elsewhere.

Article III. Members.

Section 1. The members of the Corporation shall consist of the incorporators, and such other natural persons as may be elected to membership as hereinafter provided.

Section 2. Any natural person may become a member upon election by a majority vote of the directors present at any meeting of the Board at which a quorum is present; or upon election by a majority vote of the members present at any meeting of members at which a quorum is present; or upon unanimous election in writing signed by all the then members of the Corporation, and filed with the Secretary.

Section 3. Members may be suspended or expelled from the Corporation, by the vote of a majority of the directors present at any meeting of the Board at which a quorum is present, or by the vote of a majority of the members present at any meeting of members at which a quorum is present, for refusing or failing to comply with the By-laws, or for other good and sufficient cause.

Article IV. Meetings of the Members of the Corporation.

Section 1. The Corporation shall hold its annual meeting of members for the election of directors, and for the transaction of such other business as may come before the meeting, on the first Tuesday of February in each year, at a place, within or without the State of New York, and at an hour, to be specified in the notice of such meeting.

Section 2. Special meetings of members shall be called by the Secretary or an Executive Vice-President upon the request of the President or of the Board of Directors, or on the written request of one-third of the members.

Section 3. Notice of all meetings of members shall be mailed or delivered personally to each member at least two days before the meeting.

Section 4. At all meetings of members of the Corporation one-third of the members, whether present in person or by proxy, shall constitute a quorum, but less than a quorum shall have power to adjourn from time to time, until a quorum be present.

Section 5. The members may, by an instrument in writing signed by all of them, take or authorize any action which could be taken or authorized at a meeting of members.

Article V. Board of Directors.

Section 1. The number of directors shall be seventy-five; but such number may be increased or reduced, by amendment of the By-laws as hereinafter provided, within the maximum and minimum numbers fixed in the certificate of incorporation or any amendment thereto.

Section 2. The Board of Directors shall hold an annual meeting as soon as convenient after the annual meeting of the Corporation.

Other regular meetings of the Board of Directors shall be held at such times and places as the Board may determine.

Special meetings of the Board of Directors shall be called at any time by the Secretary or an Executive Vice-President upon the request of the President or of the Executive Committee or of one-fourth of the Directors then in office.

Section 3. Notice of all regular and special meetings of the Board shall be mailed or delivered personally to each director at least one day before the meeting. Meetings may be held at any place within or without the State of New York designated in the notice of the meeting.

Section 4. The Board of Directors shall have and exercise full power in the management and control of the business and affairs of the Corporation.

Section 5. Directors shall be elected by the members of the Corporation at the annual meeting or at special meetings and shall hold office until the next annual meeting and until their successors shall be elected. Vacancies occurring in the Board for any cause (including increase in the number of directors) may also be filled for the unexpired term by the majority vote of the Directors present at any meeting at which a quorum is present.

Section 6. One-third of the Board shall be necessary to constitute a quorum, but less than a quorum shall have power to adjourn from time to time until a quorum be present.

Article VI.   Committees.

Section 1. There may be an Executive Committee consisting of such number of members of the Board of Directors as the Board may from time to time determine. The President shall, ex officio, be a member and the Chairman of the Executive Committee. Other members of the Committee will be elected at the annual meeting or at regular or special meetings of the Board of Directors to hold office until the next annual meeting and until their successors are elected. In case of a vacancy, the same may be filled by the Board of Directors at any meeting, or, in the interim between meetings of the Board, may be filled temporarily by vote of a majority of the then members of the Executive Committee.

Section 2. The Executive Committee shall fix its own rules of procedure. Meetings of the Executive Committee shall be held at such times and places as it may determine. Notice of all meetings shall be mailed or delivered personally to each member of the Executive Committee at least one day before the meeting. A quorum for the transaction of the business of the Executive Committee shall consist of one-third of its members then in office.

Section 3. Subject to the direction of the Board of Directors, the Executive Committee shall have the immediate charge, management and control of the activities and affairs of the Corporation, and it shall have full power, in the intervals between the meetings of the Board of Directors, to do any and all things in relation to the affairs of the Corporation and to exercise any powers of the Board of Directors which are not specifically contemplated by law or these By-laws to be exercised by the directors acting through the Board of Directors as such.

Section 4. The Board of Directors or the Executive Committee may appoint a Budget Committee. Except as otherwise resolved by the Board of Directors or the Executive Committee, the Budget Committee will prepare and submit to the Board of Directors or the Executive Committee from time to time as requested, budgets and plans for the carrying out of the purposes of the Corporation, the financial requirements of the Corporation in respect thereof, the provision or raising of funds to meet such requirements, and the allocation of the funds and resources of the Corporation to such purposes, either directly or through other eligible corporations, organizations and bodies. The Budget Committee, if and to the extent authorized by the Board of Directors or the Executive Committee, may exercise powers, duties and advisory functions in relation to eligibility and other matters referred to in Section 2 of Article I; and, in addition, shall have such other powers, duties and advisory functions as may be conferred upon it from time to time by the By-laws or by the Board of Directors or the Executive Committee.

Section 5. The Board of Directors or the Executive Committee may appoint from time to time, a Campaign Committee, a Committee on Public Relations, and such other Committees as the Board of Directors or the Executive Committee may deem advisable, and each such Committee shall exercise such powers and perform such duties as may be conferred upon it by the Board of Directors or the Executive Committee, subject to the continuing direction and control of the Board of Directors and the Executive Committee.

Article VII. Officers.

Section 1. The elected officers of the Corporation shall consist of a President, one or more Vice-Presidents, a Secretary, and a Treasurer.

Section 2. The appointed officers of the Corporation shall be such Executive Vice-Presidents, Assistant Vice-Presidents, Assistant Secretaries, Assistant Treasurers and Signing Officers, as the Board of Directors or the Executive Committee may from time to time determine to appoint.

Section 3. The Board of Directors or the Executive Committee shall have power at any time to create additional offices.

Section 4. The President shall be the chief executive officer of the Corporation, and shall be in charge of the direction of its affairs. The Executive Vice-President or Executive Vice-Presidents shall be the active administrative officer or officers of the Corporation, and charged with the administration of its activities, subject to the direction of the Board of Directors and the respective Committees and the President. The Executive Vice-President or Executive Vice-Presidents shall make such reports to the Board and to the several Committees, and to the President, as may from time to time be requested; and shall have such other powers and perform such other duties as may from time to time be prescribed by the Board of Directors or the Executive Committee. The other officers of the Corporation shall have the powers and perform the duties that usually pertain to their respective offices, or as may from time to time be prescribed by the Board of Directors or the Executive Committee.

Section 5. The elected officers and the directors shall not receive, directly or indirectly, any salary or other compensation from the Corporation, unless authorized by the concurring vote of two-thirds of all the directors. Appointed officers are authorized to receive such compensation as may from time to time be determined by the Board of Directors or the Executive Committee.

Section 6. The elected officers shall be elected at the annual meeting or at regular or special meetings of the Board of Directors, and the appointed officers shall be appointed at the annual meeting or at regular or special meetings of the Board of Directors, or by the Executive Committee. All officers shall hold office until the next annual meeting and until their successors are elected or until removed by action of a body which, under these By-laws, has the power to elect or appoint them.

Section 7. All officers and other persons who may be authorized by the Board of Directors or any Committee thereof, to receive or disburse funds of the Corporation, shall be required to furnish bonds for the faithful discharge of their duties, in such sums and with such surety and on such conditions as the Board or such Committee shall from time to time determine or authorize. The expenses of such bonds shall be borne by the Corporation.

Section 8. After the close of each fiscal year of the Corporation, beginning with that ending December 31, 1943, the financial transactions of the Corporation for the preceding fiscal year shall be audited by independent auditors as directed by the Board of Directors or the Executive Committee and a report of the audit shall be made to the Board of Directors or the Executive Committee.

Article VIII. *Fiscal Year.*

Section 1. The fiscal year of the Corporation shall be the calendar year.

Article IX. *Seal.*

Section 1. The seal of the Corporation shall be circular in form and shall bear the name of the Corporation and the year of its incorporation.

Article X. *Amendments.*

Section 1. These By-laws may be added to, amended or repealed, in whole or in part, by the members or by the Board of Directors or by the Executive Committee, in each case by a majority vote at any meeting at which a quorum is present, provided that notice of the proposed addition, amendment or repeal has been given to each member, or director, or member of the Executive Committee, as the case may be, in the notice of such meeting. In the event of any conflict between the By-laws as added to, amended or repealed by the Board of Directors or by the Executive Committee, and the By-laws as added to, amended or repealed by the members, the By-laws as added to, amended or repealed by the members shall prevail; and in the event of any conflict between the By-laws as added to, amended or repealed by the Executive Committee and the By-laws as added to, amended or repealed by the Board of Directors, the By-laws as added to, amended or repealed by the Board of Directors shall prevail.

Appendix B

MEMORANDUM OF AGREEMENT between NATIONAL WAR FUND, INC., a New York corporation (hereinafter called the "Fund") and. . . . .
. . . .
. . . .
a. corporation hereinafter called the "Agency").
In recognition of the fact that unification of the fund-raising activities of the numerous war relief and service agencies is desirable in the interest of the contributing public and such agencies, the Fund has been organized, at the recommendation of The President's War Relief Control Board, to conduct in a single coordinated program all fund-raising activities on behalf of such war-related agencies other than the American National Red Cross. For the purpose of facilitating that full cooperation which is essential to the successful carrying out of the joint enterprise, between the Fund and those agencies (hereinafter called "Participating Agencies") which shall agree to participate in such program by executing agreements with the Fund substantially similar to this agreement, and in consideration of the mutual obligations herein expressed, the Fund and the Agency agree as follows:

CAMPAIGNS AND SOLICITATIONS

1. The Agency designates the Fund as its sole representative for all fund-raising activities in the United States and its possessions on behalf of the Agency.

2. The Fund assumes responsibility for such fund-raising on behalf of the Agency and will use its best efforts to obtain for the Agency such sums as may be necessary to meet the net operating requirements of the Agency for the years 1943 and 1944, as contained in its approved budget.

3. The Fund will conduct during the Fall of 1943 a nationwide public campaign for contributions for the support of the Agency and of the other Participating Agencies, together with such other solicitations and other fund-raising activities as the Fund shall deem desirable from time to time. Such campaigns and solicitations will be conducted, when possible, through or in collaboration with state war chests, community chests and other local campaign units designated or approved by the Fund as part of a single coordinated fund-raising effort. The nature and conduct of all such campaigns and solicitations on behalf of the Agency will be subject to the sole determination and direction of the Fund.

4. In order to avoid interference with the efforts of the Fund on behalf of all Participating Agencies, the Agency will not hereafter engage in any fund-raising activities in the United States of any character whatsoever (including solicitations of contributions and benefits, entertainments and commercial undertakings for the raising of funds) except with the prior approval of and under arrangements made directly with the Fund or its

designated representative or except as provided in paragraph 5. The Agency shall notify the Fund promptly of any campaign or other fund-raising activities on its behalf now in progress or organized, and any such activities shall be terminated at a time fixed by the Fund.

5. Local committees or other local representatives of the Agency may continue activities heretofore conducted by them on a regular basis for the purpose of sustaining local interest in the Agency even though such activities may incidentally involve fund-raising activities, but in all such cases the prior approval of the local campaign representative of the Fund should be obtained.

6. The Agency may continue to accept unsolicited cash contributions and renewals of membership dues, but all amounts so received by the Agency shall be taken into account in determining the net operating requirements of the Agency which are to be met by the Fund. The Agency may also continue to accept and to solicit contributions in kind.

7. The Agency will cooperate to the fullest possible extent in the campaign activities of the Fund. In this connection it will use its best efforts to secure the active participation in the campaign of its local committees and other representatives, and will make available to the Fund its facilities and all such information with respect to its activities and all other campaign material as the Fund shall request.

APPROVAL OF BUDGETS

8. When requested by the Budget Committee of the Fund, the Agency will submit to it the budgets of the Agency for the years 1943 and 1944, together with all such necessary supporting data in connection therewith as may be desirable. The Agency will be afforded full opportunity to discuss such budgets with representatives of the Budget Committee. The recommendations of the Budget Committee will be submitted to the Board of Directors or Executive Committee of the Fund for approval.

9. The approved budget of the Agency as above determined and any allotments based thereon may be modified by the Board of Directors or Executive Committee of the Fund, after discussion with the Agency, in the event of any under-subscription to the campaign goal of the Fund. Such allotments may also be so modified prior to payment to the Agency when necessary to give proper effect to a reduction in the net operating requirements of the Agency resulting from a lessening of needs, an increase in related governmental relief activities or other like factors. The Agency may at any time apply to the Budget Committee of the Fund for additional allotments where it deems such action necessary or desirable.

10. The Board of Directors or Executive Committee of the Fund, acting upon the recommendation of the Budget Committee, will determine the list of Participating Agencies on whose behalf fund-raising activities will be conducted by the Fund, the approved budgets of all such agencies to be included in the campaign goal of the Fund and the amount of the total campaign goal of the Fund.

11. No charge will be made to the Agency for campaign and collection costs. The Fund will include in its campaign goal an amount deemed

sufficient to cover all such costs and all costs of operation of the Fund, together with reasonable provision for non-payment of pledges.

12. The Fund may also include in its campaign goal provision for a contingent fund in such amount as the Fund shall determine. Such contingent fund will be applied by the Fund as hereinafter provided.

13. Contributors will be accorded the privilege of designating the Agency as the recipient of all or a part of their contributions. Such designations will be recognized by the Fund, but the Fund reserves the right to request all or any of such contributors to modify or rescind such designations if the Agency would otherwise receive an amount in excess of its approved budget. The designation in any campaign goal of the Fund or of any state war chest or local campaign unit of amounts as allocable to the Agency shall not give to the Agency the right to receive moneys in such amounts from the Fund or otherwise alter the right of the Agency to receive moneys from the Fund as specified herein.

DISPOSITION OF MONEYS RECEIVED BY THE FUND

14. Campaign and collection costs and all other costs of operation of the Fund shall constitute a first charge against sums received by the Fund, and the Fund shall be entitled to reserve out of moneys so received by it such amounts as it shall deem necessary therefor before making payments to the Agency.

15. To the extent that, in the opinion of the Board of Directors or Executive Committee of the Fund, the cash resources of the Fund and its obligations to all Participating Agencies permit, the Fund will pay to the Agency monthly an amount sufficient to meet its current net operating requirements, as approved by the Fund. Such net operating requirements shall be the amount by which the approved cash disbursements of the Agency exceed its cash receipts from all sources other than the Fund, including in such receipts all cash on hand and income from trust and other funds except any such cash or income as shall, under the terms of the gift, be unavailable for the operating requirements of the Agency. For such purpose, the Agency shall file monthly with the Fund appropriate statements of its receipts and disbursements.

16. Amounts allocated by the Fund to the contingent fund, and any amounts received by the Fund in excess of its campaign goals, may be temporarily retained by the Fund or disbursed by it, from time to time, for the purpose of supplying funds for the work of any war relief or service agencies not originally included in the Participating Agencies because of their minor character, for meeting the increased needs of any Participating Agencies, and for such other purposes as shall be approved by the Board of Directors or Executive Committee of the Fund.

17. Within the limits of its approved budget, the Agency shall determine the distribution to be made by it of all moneys received by it from the Fund, except that where major changes are proposed in the amount or purposes of such distribution from those specified in its approved budget, the Agency shall obtain the approval of the Budget Committee of the Fund to such modifications. In particular, in order to preserve the deductibility

for tax purposes of contributions to the Fund, no funds received by the agency from the Fund shall be expended for purposes not of a character described in the applicable provisions of the federal income tax law.

GENERAL

18. The Agency will file with the Fund a copy of each audited statement of its account filed by it with The President's War Relief Control Board and will supply to the Fund, from time to time, all such other information concerning its affairs as the Fund may reasonably request.

19. The Fund assumes the responsibility of supplying to state war chests and local campaign units all necessary information concerning the budgets and activities of the Agency. The Fund will also arrange for the filing with governmental bodies of such reports as may be required with respect to fund-raising activities on behalf of the Agency conducted by the Fund or its representatives.

20. If the Agency shall be dissolved or otherwise cease to carry on the activities contemplated in its approved budget, all funds then held by the Agency or subsequently received by it (whether as contributions or upon the sale or other disposition of property held by it or otherwise) which are not required to pay or provide for the payment of outstanding obligations and commitments of the Agency, shall be repaid to the Fund at its request and the Agency shall cease to have any further interest in such funds. If at any time the Agency shall hold any excess funds not reasonably required to meet its net operating requirements, it shall, when requested by the Fund, pay over such excess funds to the Fund to be held by it in its contingent fund.

21. If the Fund shall be dissolved or otherwise cease to carry on its activities on behalf of the Participating Agencies as provided herein and in similar agreements entered into with such Agencies, it shall with all reasonable promptness pay over to any successor organization, or to the Participating Agencies in such proportions as the Board of Directors or Executive Committee of the Fund shall determine, all funds then held or subsequently received by the Fund which are not required to pay or provide for the payment of outstanding obligations and commitments of the Fund.

22. This agreement shall continue in full force and effect until December 31, 1944 and thereafter until such date as shall be designated by the Fund or the Agency in a written notice, delivered to the other party, of its election to terminate this agreement, such date to be not less than ninety days following the delivery of such notice.

NATIONAL WAR FUND, INC.

Dated: , 1943

By ....
                                                    President

By ....

....

....

                                                    President

Appendix C

MEMORANDUM OF AGREEMENT between NATIONAL WAR FUND, INC., a New York corporation (hereinafter called the "Fund") and...........
..........................., a ....
corporation (hereinafter called the "State War Chest").

The Fund has been organized, at the recommendation of the President's War Relief Control Board, for the purpose of coordinating in a single national program the fund-raising activities of participating war relief and service agencies (hereinafter called the "Participating Agencies"). The State War Chest has been formed to conduct and supervise, as part of such national program, all fund-raising activities on behalf of the Participating Agencies in the State of....................... (hereinafter called the "State").

For the purpose of securing the full cooperation between the Fund and the State War Chest which is essential to the success of the program, the parties hereto have agreed together as follows:

CAMPAIGN

1. The Fund designates the State War Chest as the sole fund-raising representative in the State on behalf of the Fund and the Participating Agencies. The State War Chest accepts such designation and assumes responsibility for such activities in the State.

2. The State War Chest will conduct during each year a public campaign throughout the State for contributions for the support of the Fund and the Participating Agencies. Such campaigns will be conducted through such existing community chests or other existing local fund-raising bodies, to the extent possible, and by such other committees, groups or individuals, as shall be designated by the State War Chest and approved by the Fund for such purpose (hereinafter called the "local campaign units").

3. Neither the Fund nor the Participating Agencies will conduct, or authorize others to conduct, within the State any campaigns or other fund-raising activities on their behalf (including solicitations of contributions and benefits, entertainments and commercial undertakings for the raising of funds), except with the prior approval of the State War Chest. The Participating Agencies may, however, continue to accept unsolicited cash contributions and renewals of membership dues and to accept and solicit contributions in kind. In addition, local committees or other local representatives of the Participating Agencies may continue activities heretofore conducted by them on a regular basis for the purpose of sustaining local interest in the Participating Agencies, even though such activities may incidentally involve fund-raising activities, subject to the approval of the local campaign unit.

4. In the case of certain corporations and other business and charitable

151

organizations, the Fund may solicit contributions on a national basis. The Fund will credit against the quota of the State War Chest its proper portion of any such contributions received by the Fund and will advise the State War Chest of any amounts so credited. No such solicitations will be undertaken by the Fund with respect to any such organization having its principal office in or otherwise particularly identified with a community within the State without prior consultation with the State War Chest or appropriate local campaign unit.

5. The Fund will conduct a national press, radio and advertising campaign in support of the efforts of the State War Chest and similar bodies in other states and will make available to the State War Chest the counsel and assistance of representatives of the campaign division of the Fund. It will keep the State War Chest currently advised with respect to activities and budgets of the Participating Agencies and the progress of the national campaign. The Fund will also make available to the State War Chest and its local campaign units, at cost, general campaign literature prepared by the Fund and the Participating Agencies. In general, the Fund will cooperate to the fullest possible extent with the campaign activities of the State War Chest and its local campaign units.

6. The State War Chest will, to the fullest possible extent, coordinate its campaign and other fund-raising activities with the national campaign organized by the Fund to be held in the fall of the year and will consult with the campaign committee of the Fund with respect to the planning and carrying out of its campaign activities. In carrying on its activities it will conform to such campaign policies with respect to benefits, commercial undertakings and similar matters as shall be announced by the Fund in the interests of uniformity in its national campaign.

QUOTAS

7. The State War Chest accepts a quota of $ . . . . for the State for the 1943 campaign. The state quotas for future years will be set by agreement between the Fund and the State War Chest.

8. In fixing the state campaign goal, the State War Chest will add to the state quota as above determined, an amount to cover its approved state campaign and administrative costs and a reasonable allowance for uncollectible pledges. It will also add any such amounts as shall be approved as hereinafter provided to meet the budgets of state-wide philanthropic organizations to be included in the unified campaign.

9. The state campaign goal so fixed will be distributed by the State War Chest to the local campaign units in the State as local campaign quotas. In making such distribution, the State War Chest will be guided by the quota system percentages recommended by the Fund and any substantial departures therefrom discussed in advance with the national campaign committee of the Fund. The total of the local campaign quotas so distributed should not exceed approximately 105% of the state campaign goal.

10. The State War Chest and its local campaign units may include in

their respective campaign goals the approved budgets of state-wide or local philanthropic organizations, provided that such organizations are of such character that contributions thereto are deductible in determining federal income taxes. Except as provided below, only already established, voluntary, non-governmental organizations may be so included and the approved budget included in the campaign goal with respect to each such organization should approximate its past budget requirements. The budgets of such organizations will be carefully reviewed by the State War Chest or local campaign unit, as the case may be, before approval and inclusion in the state or local campaign goal. Before including a newly created organization or any substantial increase in the budget of an existing organization in its local campaign goal, the local campaign unit shall obtain the approval of the State War Chest. In like instances in the case of state-wide organizations, the approval of the Fund shall be obtained.

11. Contributors will be accorded the privilege of designating one or more Participating Agencies as the recipients of all or a part of their contributions. Such designations will be recognized by the Fund, but the Fund reserves the right to request any of such contributors to modify or rescind such designations where deemed desirable.

12. The State War Chest and the local campaign units may, in fixing their campaign goals, designate amounts of their quotas as allocable to particular Participating Agencies, but such designations shall not require that the Fund distribute amounts so designated to such Agencies when, in its judgment, to do so would be inequitable or tend to result in a division of the total available funds among the Participating Agencies in a manner not in accord with their relative needs.

COLLECTION AND DISBURSEMENT OF FUNDS

13. The Treasurer of the State War Chest will make all collections of funds from local campaign units in the State, and will pay over such funds, after proper deductions for organization and campaign costs and the approved budgets of state-wide philanthropic organizations, to the Fund at such reasonable intervals as shall be agreed upon by him and the Treasurer of the Fund. All such payments will be made as promptly as practicable and, in any event, prior to the first day of October of the year following that in which the campaign is held.

14. The State War Chest will finance its own organization and campaign costs. Such costs shall be held to a reasonable figure to be established in consultation with the Fund. The amount of such approved campaign and collection costs and the year-round administrative costs of the State War Chest shall constitute a first charge against sums received by the State War Chest and it shall be entitled to reserve out of moneys received by it such amounts as are necessary therefor before making payments to the Fund.

15. If the state campaign shall have included an appeal on behalf of state-wide philanthropic organizations as well as the Participating Agencies, and should the state campaign fail of its goal by 5% or less, the net funds

received by the State War Chest remaining after deducting approved campaign and administrative expenses will be prorated between the Fund and the state-wide organizations on the basis of the respective amounts included in the state campaign goal with respect thereto. If such failure exceeds 5%, the terms of appropriation will be subject to reconsideration by the budget committee of the State War Chest after discussion with the Fund. The State War Chest recognizes that, in the event of an oversubscription, the Fund has its equitable interest in such overage which will need to be given consideration at least to the extent of its prorata interest in the total campaign goal of the State War Chest.

RELATION WITH LOCAL CAMPAIGN UNITS

16. The State War Chest will enter into appropriate agreements with each local campaign unit within the State with respect to its participation in the unified campaign. Each such agreement will provide, among other things, for the acceptance by such local campaign unit of its local campaign quota as distributed to it by the State War Chest, for an annual audit of its accounts by a certified public accountant in good standing and the filing of a copy of such audit with the State War Chest, for the prompt payment to the State War Chest of all amounts so payable, for the treatment of over and under subscriptions and the admission into the campaign of local philanthropic organizations in the manner herein provided, for the filing of such information and reports with respect to its activities and for such other matters as the State War Chest shall deem necessary or desirable in order to secure the successful operation of the local campaign as a part of the state campaign and the national campaign of the Fund. The State War Chest will furnish to the Fund a copy of each such agreement entered into with a local campaign unit.

17. The campaign and administrative expenses of the local campaign unit shall be a first charge against funds collected by it. In cases where the local campaign has been made exclusively on behalf of the State War Chest, the treasurer of the local campaign unit will remit the balance of all contributions, after such expenses, to the treasurer of the State War Chest. In cases where the local campaign has included local philanthropic organizations as well as the State War Chest, if the local campaign shall fail of its goal by 5% or less, the State War Chest and the local charities will be expected to share such under-subscription in proportion to the respective amounts included with respect to them in the local campaign goal. If such under-subscription exceeds 5%, the budget committee of the local campaign unit will review the budgets and discuss with the State War Chest the terms by which a further adjustment is to be made. In the event of an over-subscription it should be recognized that the Fund has its equitable interest in such an overage which will need to be given consideration.

GENERAL

18. The State War Chest will make such reports to the Fund with respect to its activities, the local campaign units designated by it for the

State campaign and the personnel thereof, the quotas assigned to such local campaign units and their campaign goals, the results of its campaign, and all such other matters as the Fund shall reasonably request.

19. The State War Chest will maintain uniform fiscal records to be developed in cooperation with the Treasurer of the Fund, which will be open for inspection or audit by the Fund. It will have its accounts audited at least annually by a certified public accountant in good standing and will furnish the Fund with a copy of such audited statements.

20. All employees of the State War Chest handling cash will be bonded in appropriate amounts.

21. The Fund has registered with the President's War Relief Control Board. By action of such Board, such registration includes the State War Chest and all local campaign units approved by it and no separate registration by them is required. The State War Chest will comply with any applicable regulations of such Board and, for the purpose of preparing the necessary financial reports of the Fund to be filed with the Board, the State War Chest will deliver to the Fund annually a consolidated report of the receipts and disbursements of the State War Chest and all its local campaign units within the State. The State War Chest will also supply to the Fund or the Board from time to time all such additional data as may be required by the Board in connection with the activities of the State War Chest and its local campaign units.

22. The State War Chest will arrange for the filing with any officials or other governmental bodies within the State of such reports and other documents as may be required with respect to fund-raising activities within the State. The Fund will supply to the State War Chest any such information as it may require in connection therewith.

23. If the State War Chest shall be dissolved or otherwise cease to carry on the activities contemplated in this agreement, it shall with all reasonable promptness pay over to the Fund or to any successor organization in the State designated by the Fund, all funds then held or subsequently received by the State War Chest which are not required to pay or provide for the payment of outstanding obligations and commitments of the State War Chest.

24. This agreement shall continue in full force and effect until December 31, 1944 and thereafter until such date as shall be designated by the Fund or the State War Chest in a written notice delivered to the other party of its election to terminate this agreement, such date to be not less than ninety days following the delivery of such notice.

Dated: ...., 1943

NATIONAL WAR FUND, INC.

By ....

....

By ....

Appendix D

SUGGESTED PROCEDURE
FOR
STATE CAMPAIGN ORGANIZATION

Thomas Jefferson himself would certainly approve the basic policy of the National War Fund—that every sovereign state has the right to decide how it wishes to organize to raise its share of the National War Fund's total goal.

But certain rules of common sense and practical experience hold true everywhere, and responsible people tell us that it is information they want. So the National War Fund, borrowing heavily on the successful record of the USO and other national agencies, and on the advice of local leaders throughout the country, has prepared this leaflet for your consideration and guidance. We hope you'll like it, and find it helpful.

One thing we can all be sure of: that the success of the National War Fund everywhere—North, East, South and West—will depend on these five basic essentials:

1. Active and influential leadership, backed by competent staff.
2. Representative organization.
3. Substantial adherence to the common quota system.
4. Careful planning by states, counties and local communities.
5. Broad coverage, with everybody giving, in due proportion to his means.

Whatever you do, please keep those five essentials before you. And remember too that the National War Fund is ready to serve you in every possible way.

The particulars are inside.

PRESCOTT S. BUSH
National Campaign Chairman

FIRST, HERE ARE THE ESSENTIAL FACTS

Whatever form of organization your state prefers, whether it be simply a state committee of the National War Fund or a full-fledged state war chest, there are certain fundamentals which in the common interest must apply in all states.

1. *Quotas.* The quota system adopted by the National War Fund, establishing for each state a percentage of a national goal, and suggesting in turn a county percentage of each state goal, represents many months of careful calculation, and a number of carefully selected statistical factors. Everyone can feel assured that it is fair, and as accurate as any such study can be. Every national agency associated with the National War Fund, in-

156

cluding Community Chests and Councils, Inc., has helped draw it up, and has approved it for 1943. Quotas are now ready for distribution.

Each state will be expected (1) to assume the responsibility for its state quota, (2) to add to the national figure whatever sum it may consider necessary or advisable, for state campaign and administrative expenses, and for the approved budgets of state-wide philanthropies it may wish to include in the unified appeal, and (3) to apportion the total figure in quotas for its counties. (In the apportionment to the counties, each state should weigh carefully the county percentages recommended by the National War Fund, and should see that the combined total of all county quotas includes a safety factor of approximately 5 per cent of the total state budget.)

Each state will be expected to execute a simple agreement with the National War Fund, covering the acceptance of its state quota, and in turn will also be expected to secure from its own counties or local units agreements accepting the county or local quotas. (These acceptance forms should be prepared in cooperation with, and copies of the signed forms forwarded to, the National War Fund.)

2. *Designations.* Each state, each county, each community, and each individual contributor will have the opportunity to designate more or less to any particular agency participating in the National War Fund; provided, of course, that such designations do not reduce the total assigned quota, or the amount of the individual gift.

3. *Additional Appeals.* States, counties and local communities can include the appeals of other established philanthropic agencies at their own discretion; provided that such appeals qualify for tax deductibility under Section 23 (O) or Section 23 (Q) of the Internal Revenue Code. State-wide agency admissions should be approved by the National War Fund, and local agency admissions should be approved by state committees.

Generally speaking, only voluntary non-governmental agencies should be permitted to participate.

The national agencies are responsible for the local operations and expenses of their local committees, and other bodies carrying out locally the work of the national agencies. Therefore, it will not be necessary for local campaign committees to add an amount to the National War Fund quota for these purposes. A local committee of a national war-related agency participating in the National War Fund will be expected to receive its funds for the local work of the national agency from the national agency itself.

4. *State Financing.* Each state war chest will be expected to finance its own organization, and its own costs of fund-raising and publicity. Such costs should be held to a reasonable figure, and established in consultation with the National War Fund.

State committees of the National War Fund, on the other hand, will be financed by the National War Fund, with an appropriate adjustment in the state goal, as explained in paragraph 2 of the section on Quotas.

5. *Timing.* It is hoped that communities will hold their local campaigns in the Fall, at the time when the National War Fund publicity will be at its peak, and when all communities will have the benefit of a unified

effort in all parts of the country. It is recognized, however, that for the present some variations are to be expected, and that a few local campaigns will be carried on during the Spring and Summer.

Generally, it is expected that each state will have organized either a state war chest affiliated with the National War Fund, or a state committee of the National War Fund, on or before May first.

In turn, it is expected that each state will have recruited all its district leaders by June first, all its county chairmen by July 15, and all its community or township chairmen by Labor Day.

6. *Professional Staff.*   State war chests will employ their own staffs, in consultation with the National War Fund.

State committees of the National War Fund will be provided with staff by the National War Fund, in consultation with the state authorities.

In addition, as a measure of economical management, the National War Fund will provide a few special field representatives for consultation in all states.

7. *Campaign Materials.*   The National War Fund will make available campaign supplies and publicity material for campaigns in "non-chest" areas and communities.

8. *"Overs and Unders".*   The National War Fund agrees with experienced community chest executives that problems arising from overages and shortages in fund-raising campaigns may safely be left to the fair-minded judgment of representative budget committees.

Recognizing, however, that certain basic standards must apply everywhere, the following procedures, adopted after long discussions with leaders in many states, represent the present policy of the National War Fund:

A. *Between State and National.*

The state treasurer, on receipt of funds from county and local committees, will first deduct approved campaign and administration expenses.

Should the state campaign fail by less than five per cent, proration between the National War Fund quota and state-wide agencies' quota is expected. If, however, the failure exceeds five per cent, the terms by which appropriations are to be made will be subject to reconsideration by the state budget committee.

In the event of an over-subscription, it should be recognized that the National War Fund has its equitable interest in such an overage, which will need to be given consideration, at least to the extent of its pro-rata interest in the total budget.

B. *Between State and Community.*

Within a state, campaigns may be of two types: (1) an appeal on behalf of the state War Fund or State Committee of the National War Fund exclusively, or (2) a combination of state war appeal with the local chest appeal or some other type of local appeal.

a. *Procedure for local campaign exclusively on behalf of State War Fund or State Committee of the National War Fund.*   The county or local treasurer will deduct from his receipts the amount of the approved campaign expenses and remit the balance to the state treasurer.

b. *Procedure for local campaign on behalf of the State War Fund combined with local community chest or other local appeal.*

    aa. Deduct campaign expenses first.

    bb. Should the local joint campaign fail by less than five per cent, the State War Fund quota and local budgets are expected to share proportionately the under-subscription. If, however, the undersubscription exceeds five per cent, the local budget committee will review the budgets, and then discuss with the state committee the terms by which a further adjustment is to be made.

    cc. In the event of an over-subscription, it should be recognized that the National War Fund has its equitable interest in such an overage, which will need to be given consideration.

9. *Accountability.* The state treasurer will be asked to file reports with and forward balances due to the Treasurer of the National War Fund at intervals agreed upon, and in all instances as soon as possible. In no case should the final payment be made later than October 1, 1944.

Each state is asked to maintain uniform fiscal records to be worked out in cooperation with the Treasurer of the National War Fund, and have its accounts audited annually by a certified public accountant in good standing. A copy of such audit should be forwarded to the Treasurer of the National War Fund. All employees handling state cash should be bonded.

SECOND, HERE IS THE STATE JOB

Whether a state committee or a state war chest, the state organization has no easy task. In general, its job is to see that the state quota is raised, and forwarded promptly to the National War Fund.

In particular, it has seven special functions:

1. Sponsorship for the National War Fund appeal throughout the state, with continuous interpretation of national and state policy.

2. Establishment of procedures for reviewing state-wide appeals, for fixing the total state budget, and for consulting with local committees on their budgetary problems.

3. Distribution of the state quota on an equitable basis to the campaign committees within the state and completion of signed agreements covering amount of quota and area of solicitation.

4. Organizing county and local campaigns throughout the state. (The only fund-raising any state may wish to do on a state level will probably be the solicitation of a few selected corporations doing a state-wide business, with which local appeals are considered ineffective.)

5. Development of state publicity program, coordinated with plans of publicity department at national headquarters.

6. Service to county and local committees on supplies, information, etc.

7. Collection of funds from local treasurers, and transmission to national headquarters.

THIRD, HERE IS THE SUGGESTED STATE PROCEDURE

Representatives of the National War Fund are now available to help each state with the first steps of organization.

Listed here, however, is a simple procedure already found to be practical by experience, and involving three general steps in this order:

Step One—Planning

The first move should be to call an organizing meeting of a relatively few experienced people to discuss a general plan of procedure.

Attending this initial meeting should be a few of the leading chest executives within the state, the 1942 state campaign chairmen for the USO and other national war-related appeals with experience within the state, representatives of organized labor (where available), one or two representatives from "non-chest" areas within the state, one or two business leaders with state-wide interests and contacts, a lawyer versed in state laws applying to the procedure, and a field representative of the National War Fund.

The business to be covered should include the following:

1. General plan of organization, with tentative selection of district chairmen, under whom groups of counties can be organized later. (See accompanying chart, as basis for discussion.)

2. Selections for state campaign committee. This committee should be broadly representative in terms of race, creed, occupational interest and the geographical distribution of the state's population. Specifically, consideration should be given to the following sources of membership:
   a. Leaders of state constituencies of USO and other national war-related agencies.
   b. State chamber of commerce.
   c. State directors of agricultural extension, or other officials with direct access to county farm agents.
   d. State-wide business interests, such as the telephone company, banking associations, public utilities, and the like.
   e. Leading community chest executives.
   f. Organized labor.
   g. Religious bodies.
   h. State avenues of publicity; such as press associations, publishers, radio stations, and the like.
   i. All district chairmen.

3. Selections for state offices; permanent or acting state campaign chairman, treasurer, secretary, chairmen of state sub-committees, etc.

4. Selection of professional state campaign director.

5. Provisions for financing. (If necessary.)

6. Date and place for first meeting of state campaign committee.

(In the event the decision has not already been made, this organization meeting should also discuss the alternatives of setting up either a state committee of the National War Fund or a State War Chest affiliated with the National War Fund.)

Step Two—Leadership

Between the original meeting, and the first meeting of the state campaign committee, the acting chairman should explore the questions of campaign leadership in consultation with the field staff of the National War Fund, state officers and chairmen of state sub-committees, district chairmen, and—in consultation with the National Treasurer—the state treasurer.

Staff will assist in this work, and will also be making preliminary arrangements for state headquarters.

Step Three—Formal Organization

At the first meeting of the state campaign committee, officers and committees should be appointed, the state quota should be officially accepted, and a public announcement should be made.

Thereafter, state-wide procedure will be indicated by the course of events, and can be laid out readily upon consultation with the field staff of the National War Fund.

FOURTH, HERE IS THE DISTRICT JOB

For a number of obvious reasons, including the increasing difficulties of transportation, it will be found advisable, as it was last year in Alabama, to divide the state into districts, each with a district chairman, and with a district committee comprising the county chairmen.

These districts should be determined on a basis of natural trading areas, with convenience of transportation, rather than on any political basis, such as Congressional Districts.

The principal duties of the district chairmen are as follows:

1. Appointing in each county in the district, in consultation with the state campaign chairman, an outstanding citizen to serve as county chairman. This selection should keep in mind persons who will give the necessary time to the work, and faithfully carry out their duties in organizing the town and rural committees necessary to insure thorough personal solicitation throughout the county.

2. Immediate enlistment of these county chairmen and subsequent follow-through to see that each one has his organization completed by Labor Day.

3. Arrangements for a general meeting of all county chairmen at some central point to discuss organization procedure as outlined by the national and state committees. The county chairmen must be provided with full information and instructions in order to secure effective results. The state chairman should attend this meeting, along with the state campaign director, to give assistance and counsel.

4. Preparation of information so that the state committee is advised of all planning within the district and is given a complete record of all county chairmen and any additional members of the district committee.

5. Analysis of reports from the county chairmen, forwarded from state headquarters, and assistance to those committees that may need help to bring their campaigns to a successful conclusion.

County chairmen should constitute the membership of the district committee. However, other members may be added; such as, newspaper and radio men in the district, along with prominent speakers who will assist in informing the citizens of the area on the importance of the war fund appeal. It is suggested that a list of the best speakers within the district be supplied to state headquarters in view of their being used in other meetings in the state.

FIFTH, HERE IS THE AVAILABLE MATERIAL

To help each state do its work easily and well, each state chairman should make sure that he is supplied with the following information from the National War Fund:

1. Quota studies, to assist in the assignment of equitable quotas to the campaign committees within the state.

2. Memorandum of Understanding, covering arrangements with the campaign committees within the state.

3. A report listing state and local campaign chairmen and amounts contributed in their areas, in so far as possible, in the 1942 campaigns of the member agencies of the National War Fund.

4. Publicity Manual.

5. Suggested Procedure for County and Local Campaign Committees.

Appendix E—Directories

Robert P. Booth
Manchester, N. H.
Lindsay Bradford
New York City
Morgan B. Brainard, Sr.
Hartford, Conn.
Dr. H. A. Brandes
Bismarck, N. D.
Philip S. Brooke
Spokane, Wash.
E. P. Brooks
Chicago, Ill.
*Thomas D'Arcy
Brophy
New York City
Henry Bruere
New York City
John Stewart Bryan
Richmond, Va.
John S. Burke
New York City
*Prescott S. Bush
New York City
George A. Butler
Houston, Texas
Hon. Charles C. Cabot
Boston, Mass.
Dr. Harmon Caldwell
Athens, Ga.
Hon. Millard F.
Caldwell
Tallahassee, Fla.
L. A. Campbell
Missoula, Mont.
*J. Herbert Case
New York City
Thomas C. Cashen
Buffalo, N. Y.
Michael J. Cleary
Milwaukee, Wis.
*John A. Coleman
New York City
Stewart J. Cort
Sparrows Point, Md.
Dr. Claybrook
Cottingham
Ruston, La.

Walter J. Cummins
Chicago, Ill.
Hon. Colgate W.
Darden, Jr.
Norfolk, Va.
Mrs. Joseph E. Davies
Washington, D. C.
Walter G. Davis
Portland, Maine
Hon. Jess C. Denious
Dodge City, Kansas
Richard R. Deupree
Cincinnati, Ohio
Franklin D'Olier
Newark, N. J.
David Dubinsky
New York City
Frank D. Eaman
Detroit, Mich.
B. M. Edwards
Columbia, S. C.
Earl B. Emrey
Atlanta, Ga.
Mark F. Ethridge
Louisville, Ky.
J. W. Farley
Boston, Mass.
Marshall Field
New York City
Charles T. Fisher, Jr.
Detroit, Mich.
Ralph T. Fisher
Oakland, Calif.
Ralph E. Flanders
Boston, Mass.
Edsel Ford
Dearborn, Mich.
Harold S. Fuller
Boston, Mass.
Parrish Fuller
Oakdale, La.
Jose M. Gallardo
Arlington, Va.
Dr. Grady Gammage
Tempe, Ariz.
Thomas S. Gates
Philadelphia, Pa.

Earl J. Glade
Salt Lake City, Utah
Charles F. Glore
Chicago, Ill.
Clarence W. Goris
Gary, Ind.
Albert S. Goss
Washington, D. C.
Joseph P. Grace
New York, N. Y.
Edwin C. Graham
Washington, D. C.
William Green
Washington, D. C.
Hon. Morley Griswold
Reno, Nevada
Robert G. Hackett
Wilmington, Dela.
Stewart F. Hancock
Syracuse, N. Y.
Robert M. Hanes
Winston-Salem, N. C.
Mrs. Basil Harris
New York City
*Ralph Hayes
Wilmington, Dela.
Walter L. Hays
Orlando, Fla.
H. J. Heinz, II
Pittsburgh, Pa.
Robert E. Lee Hill
Columbia, Mo.
Sidney Hillman
New York, N. Y.
Fred Hoke
Indianapolis, Ind.
R. Miller Holland
Owensboro, Kentucky
Sidney Hollander
Baltimore, Md.
Hon. Norwin D.
Houser
Perryville, Mo.
Walter Hoving
New York City
Palmer Hoyt
Denver, Colo.

Mrs. Henry A. Ingraham
New York City

Hon. Richard M. Jefferies
Walterboro, S. C.

Hon. W. D. Jochems
Wichita, Kansas

Alfred G. Kahn
Little Rock, Ark.

Charles F. Kennedy
Van Wert, Ohio

Thomas Kennedy
Hazleton, Pa.

Henry R. Kruse
Seattle, Wash.

William Fulton Kurtz
Philadelphia, Pa.

Thomas W. Lamont
New York, N. Y.

Howard C. Lawrence
Grand Rapids, Mich.

Richard W. Lawrence
New York City

Randall J. LeBoeuf, Jr.
New York City

Mrs. Herbert H. Lehman
Washington, D. C.

Col. T. Walker Lewis
Memphis, Tenn.

* Mrs. Oswald B. Lord
New York City

Dr. V. A. Lowry
Madison, S. D.

* Henry R. Luce
New York City

C. M. Lupfer
Balboa Heights, Canal Zone

Hon. Thomas J. Mabry
Santa Fe, N. M.

Carl C. Magee
Oklahoma City, Okla.

* Francis P. Matthews
Omaha, Nebr.

George Z. Medalie
New York City

* Aubrey H. Mellinger
Chicago, Ill.

A. L. Miller
Battle Creek, Mich.

William E. Mitchell
Atlanta, Ga.

William V. Montavon
Washington, D. C.

Philip M. Morgan
Worcester, Mass.

Mrs. Dwight W. Morrow
Englewood, N. J.

C. Hamilton Moses
Little Rock, Ark.

Dr. John R. Mott
New York City

Hon. James M. Murray, Sr.
Hobbs, N. Mex.

Philip Murray
Washington, D. C.

J. W. McAfee
St. Louis, Mo.

Major L. P. McLendon
Greensboro, N. C.

Dr. Frank L. McVey
Lexington, Ky.

* Irving S. Olds
New York City

Edward A. O'Neal III
Chicago, Ill.

Wilbert J. O'Neill
Cleveland, Ohio

James R. Page
Los Angeles, Calif.

James L. Palmer
Chicago, Ill.

Haygood Paterson
Montgomery, Ala.

W. A. Patterson
Chicago, Ill.

James G. Patton
Denver, Colo.

Edward S. Perry
Springfield, Ill.

Frank Phillips
Bartlesville, Okla.

Hon. Ben H. Powell
Austin, Texas

* Fred W. Ramsey
Cleveland, Ohio

Clarence B. Randall
Chicago, Ill.

James W. Reily
New Orleans, La.

* Gordon S. Rentschler
New York City

Dr. John H. Reynolds
Conway, Ark.

Capt. Edward V. Rickenbacker
New York City

F. H. Ricketson
Denver, Colo.

Julius A. Rippel
Newark, N. J.

* E. A. Roberts
Philadelphia, Pa.

* John D. Rockefeller, Jr.
New York City

Lessing J. Rosenwald
Jenkintown, Pa.

Frank A. Ross
Madison, Wis.

* Walter Rothschild
Brooklyn, N. Y.

Charles A. Russell
Haddam, Conn.

* Edward L. Ryerson
Chicago, Ill.

Carl O. Schmidt
Wheeling, W. Va.

Jacob F. Schoellkopf, Jr.
Buffalo, N. Y.

E. J. Schulte
Casper, Wyoming

Marcus C. Sloss
San Francisco, Calif.

Hon. *Alfred E. Smith*
New York City
Esme A. C. Smith
Rutland, Vt.
Hermon D. Smith
Chicago, Ill.
Tom K. Smith
St. Louis, Mo.
Philip E. Spalding
Honolulu, T. H.
Hon. Charles A.
Sprague
Salem, Oregon
Robert G. Sproul
Berkeley, Calif.
Arthur C. Spurr
Fairmont, W. Va.
W. A. Steadman
Montgomery, Ala.
Col. Herman W.
Steinkraus
Bridgeport, Conn.
Elmer T. Stevens
Chicago, Ill.
Robert C. Stovall
Columbus, Miss.

C. J. Strike
Boise, Idaho
Frank J. Sulloway
Concord, N. H.
*Gerard Swope
New York City
M. S. Szymczak
Washington, D. C.
Edmund Taylor
Greenville, Miss.
J. Cameron Thomson
Minneapolis, Minn.
John J. Tigert
Gainesville, Fla.
Channing H. Tobias
New York City
Harold S. Vanderbilt
New York City
Henry C. Van Schaack
Denver, Colo.
George C. Wallace
Jackson, Miss.
*Allen Wardwell
New York City
Thomas J. Watson
New York City

William W. Waymack
Des Moines, Iowa
Carl Weeks
Des Moines, Iowa
Henry J. Wheelwright
Bangor, Maine
William Allen White
Emporia, Kansas
W. Walter Williams
Seattle, Wash.
William H. Williams
Little Rock, Ark.
Hon. *William H. Wills*
Bennington, Vt.
Paul Windels
New York City
William P. Witherow
Pittsburgh, Pa.
*Matthew Woll
New York City
Thomas C. Woods
Lincoln, Nebr.
*Henry M. Wriston
Providence, R. I.

BUDGET COMMITTEE

Chairman

Gerard Swope

Abraham Bluestein
C. M. Bookman
Otto F. Bradley
Henry Bruere
J. Herbert Case
Maxwell Hahn

Ralph Hayes
Sidney Hollander
S. Whitney Landon
Philip R. Mather
William F. Montavon
Arthur Packard

Mrs. Frederick M. Paist
Leo Perlis
Julius A. Rippel
Isidor Sack
Charles E. Spencer
Monroe Sweetland

PUBLIC RELATIONS COMMITTEE

Chairman, 1943—Henry M. Wriston
Chairman, 1944-47—Thomas D'Arcy Brophy

Ralph Allum
Harry Batten
Heagan Bayles
Carl Bondus
Joseph R. Busk

Edwin Cox
John P. Cunningham
George Dearnley
Julian Field
Kerwin H. Fulton

Paul Holder
H. J. Heinz, II
Gerald Link
Edward Mante
Howard W. Newton

Herbert R. Noxon
John B. Rosebrook
Thomas J. Ross
Hubbell Robinson

Raymond Rubicam
J. Harold Ryan
John Sterling
Carl Swanson

Walter J. Weir
Harold Wengler
Cranston Williams
James W. Young

NATIONAL COMMITTEE ON CORPORATIONS

Chairman, 1943-44—Irving S. Olds
Chairman, 1945—Edward L. Ryerson

Winthrop W. Aldrich
Prescott S. Bush

J. Cheever Cowdin
W. S. S. Rodgers

Adolph Zukor

QUOTA REVIEW COMMITTEE

Chairman, 1943—J. Cameron Thomson
Chairman, 1944-45—Charles A. Russell

Ralph H. Blanchard
Prescott S. Bush
L. A. Campbell
Earl B. Emrey

William J. Flather
Dr. Grady Gammage
Robert G. Hackett
Charles F. Kennedy
Ralph E. Weeks

S. Whitney Landon
Col. T. Walker Lewis
Philip M. Morgan
B. V. Sturdivant

ADVISORY CABINET

Chairman

C. M. Bookman

Ralph H. Blanchard
Otto F. Bradley
Harry M. Carey
Robert E. Coburn
Percival Dodge

Kirk E. Latta
David Liggett
Robert O. Loosley
Robert H. MacRae
Lynn D. Mowat
Elwood Street

Kenneth Sturges
Carter Taylor
Harry P. Wareham
Terrance L. Webster
Harold E. Winey

Secretary

Carl A. Kersting

SPECIAL SERVICES COMMITTEE

Chairman
Terrance L. Webster
Columbus, Ohio

Mrs. Florence S. Adams
Birmingham, Ala.
Bevins Austin
San Francisco, Calif.

Raymond E. Baarts
Kansas City, Mo.
Abraham Bluestein
New York City

Lyscom A. Bruce
Worcester, Mass.
Gerald W. Burke
Syracuse, N. Y.

Robert E. Coburn
Chicago, Ill.
Boyce M. Edens
Atlanta, Ga.
H. L. R. Emmett
Erie, Pa.
Rudolph N. Evjen
Oklahoma City, Okla.
Edward J. Fisher
Springfield, Ill.
Joseph D. Gibbon
St. Paul, Minn.
Leonard V. Griffith
San Diego, Calif.
John L. Irwin
Springfield, Mass.
Charles F. Isackes
Lexington, Ky.
E. J. Keyes
Richmond, Va.

Walter C. Laidlaw
Detroit, Mich.
Kirk E. Latta
St. Louis, Mo.
Robert O. Loosley
Providence, R. I.
Virgil Martin
Indianapolis, Ind.
Michael F. McCaffrey
Peoria, Ill.
Richard P. Miller
Rochester, N. Y.
Hon. Cecil Morgan
Baton Rouge, La.
Leo Perlis
New York City
Paul F. Rake
Philadelphia, Pa.
Chester C. Ridge
Grand Rapids, Mich.

R. L. Sheetz
Norfolk, Va.
Seward C. Simons
Oakland, Calif.
William A. Sohl
Omaha, Nebr.
Carter Taylor
Pittsburgh, Pa.
Thomas P. Thompson
Norfolk, Va.
Wayland D. Towner
Austin, Texas
Harry P. Wareham
Rochester, N. Y.
Mrs. Jane Williams
Mansfield, Ohio
F. Glenn Wood
Cincinnati, Ohio
Thomas C. Woods
Lincoln, Nebr.

Appendix F

USO
United Seamen's Service
American Field Service
War Prisoners Aid, Inc.

* * *

Belgian War Relief Society
British War Relief Society
United China Relief
American Relief for Czechoslovakia
America Denmark Relief
U. S. Committee for the Care of
European Children

American Relief for France
Greek War Relief Association
American Relief for Holland
American Relief for Italy
United Lithuanian Relief Fund
Friends of Luxembourg
American Relief for Norway
Philippine War Relief
American Relief for Poland
Refugee Relief Trustees
Russian War Relief
United Yugoslav Relief Fund

PARTICIPATING SERVICES

American Social Hygiene
Association
Bundles for Britain
Near East Foundation
War Prisoners Aid Committee,
YMCA

War Relief Services—National
Catholic Welfare Conference
World Emergency and War
Victims Fund, YWCA
World Students Service Fund

COOPERATING ORGANIZATIONS

Labor League for Human Rights—
United Nations Relief (A F of L)

National CIO Community Services
Committee

Appendix G—State Organizations

Alabama War Chest, Inc.

PRESIDENT
Haygood Paterson (1943–46)

CHAIRMAN
A. Key Foster (1943–44)
Harwell Davis (1944–45)
Frank E. Spain (1945–46)

CO-CHAIRMAN
J. Frank Rushton (1943–44)
J. L. Bedsole (1944–45)
N. Floyd McGowin (1945–46)

TREASURER
W. C. Bowman (1943–46)

EXECUTIVE DIRECTOR
Earle C. Lackey (1943–46)

Arizona United War Fund, Inc.

PRESIDENT
Dr. Grady Gammage (1943–46)

TREASURER
Walter R. Bimson (1943–46)

EXECUTIVE DIRECTOR
Ralph E. Nollner (1943–46)

Arkansas State Committee, NWF

CHAIRMAN
Dr. J. H. Reynolds (1943–46)

CAMPAIGN CHAIRMAN
C. H. Moses (1943–46)

TREASURER
W. A. McDonnell (1943–44)
Guy Williams (1944–46)

EXECUTIVE DIRECTOR
Philo C. Dix (1943–45)
Edward L. King (1945–46)

California War Chest, Inc.

PRESIDENT
Ralph T. Fisher (1943–46)

TREASURER
John F. Forbes (1943–46)

EXECUTIVE DIRECTOR
J. Henry Lang (1943–46)

United War Chest of Colorado, Inc.

PRESIDENT
F. H. Ricketson, Jr. (1943–46)

TREASURER
Roblin H. Davis (1943–45)
Henry A. Kugeler (1945–46)

EXECUTIVE DIRECTOR

Walter S. Hopkins   (1943–46)

United War and Community Funds of Connecticut, Inc.

PRESIDENT

Milton H. Glover   (1943–45)
Col. Herman W. Steinkraus
(1945–46)

TREASURER

Abbott H. Davis   (1943–44)
John R. Daniell   (1944–46)

CHAIRMAN

Oliver V. Ober   (1943–44)
Ogden Bigelow   (1944–45)
Herbert L. Crapo   (1945–46)

EXECUTIVE DIRECTOR

A. Edward Campbell   (1943–45)
Henry Endress   (1945–46)
William P. Spear   (1945–46)

United War Fund of Delaware, Inc.

PRESIDENT

Francis V. duPont   (1943–44)
Robert G. Hackett   (1944–45)
John B. Jessup   (1945–46)

TREASURER

J. K. Garrigues   (1943–46)

EXECUTIVE DIRECTOR

L. A. Webster   (1943–46)

Community War Fund of Washington, D. C., Inc.

PRESIDENT

Edwin C. Graham   (1943–46)

TREASURER

Corcoran Thom   (1943–46)

CHAIRMAN

Coleman Jennings   (1943–45)
Lee D. Butler   (1945–46)

EXECUTIVE DIRECTOR

Herbert L. Willett, Jr.   (1943–46)

National War Fund—Florida Division

PRESIDENT

Spessard L. Holland   (1943–45)
Walter L. Hays   (1945–46)

TREASURER

D. M. Barnett   (1943–46)

CHAIRMAN

Dr. John J. Tigert   (1943–45)
Hon. Millard Caldwell
(1945–46)

EXECUTIVE DIRECTOR

Geo. A. Brautigam   (1943–46)
J. Ed. Baker   (1945–46)

United War Fund of Georgia

PRESIDENT

Earl B. Emrey   (1943–45)
Dr. Harmon W. Caldwell
(1945–46)

TREASURER

E. T. Johnson   (1943–46)

EXECUTIVE DIRECTOR
Eugene Baker (1943–46)

Idaho War Fund, Inc.

PRESIDENT
C. J. Strike (1943–46)

TREASURER
Myrtle Enking (1943–44)
Ruth Moon (1944–46)

Illinois State War Fund, Inc.

PRESIDENT
E. S. Perry (1943–44)
Kurt T. Bretscher (1944–45)
Harold W. Prehn (1945–46)

TREASURER
John L. Taylor (1943–44)
Willard Bunn, Jr. (1944–46)

CHAIRMAN
John M. Joyce (1944–45)

EXECUTIVE DIRECTOR
Orlo F. King (1943–44)
H. A. Amerman (1944–46)

Indiana War Fund, Inc.

PRESIDENT
Clarence W. Goris (1943–46)

TREASURER
Paul E. Fisher (1943–46)

EXECUTIVE DIRECTOR
Frank K. Zoll (1943–46)

Iowa War Chest, Inc.

PRESIDENT
Carl Weeks (1943–46)

TREASURER
John de Jong (1943–46)

EXECUTIVE DIRECTOR
Robert H. Caldwell (1943–45)
E. L. C. White (1945–46)

Kansas United War Fund, Inc.

PRESIDENT
Hon. Jess C. Denious (1943–44)
Hon. W. D. Jochems (1944–46)

TREASURER
David Neiswanger (1943–46)

EXECUTIVE DIRECTOR
Frank L. Bynum (1943–46)

Kentucky War Fund, Inc.

PRESIDENT
R. Miller Holland (1943–46)

TREASURER
John C. Nichols (1943–46)

CHAIRMAN
Dr. Frank L. McVey (1943–46)

EXECUTIVE DIRECTOR
Robert H. Smith, Jr. (1943–45)
Mary E. Theobald (1945–46)

United War Fund of Louisiana, Inc.

PRESIDENT

Dr. Claybrook Cottingham
(1943-44)
Parrish Fuller (1944-46)

TREASURER

A. R. Johnson   (1943-46)

EXECUTIVE DIRECTOR

Earl M. Martin   (1943-46)

Maine State War Chest, Inc.

PRESIDENT

Henry J. Wheelwright
(1943-46)

TREASURER

H. Nelson MacDougall
(1943-44)
Rolland E. Irish   (1944-46)

CHAIRMAN

Rolland E. Irish   (1943-44)
Malcolm E. Morrell   (1944-46)

EXECUTIVE DIRECTOR

Harry B. Taplin   (1943-44)
Louis W. Collier   (1944-45)
Ruth T. Clough   (1945-46)

National War Fund in Maryland, Inc.

CHAIRMAN

Stewart J. Cort   (1943-45)
W. Wallace Lanahan
(1945-46)

TREASURER

L. S. Zimmerman   (1943-46)

EXECUTIVE DIRECTOR

Victor A. Rule   (1943-46)

NWF—Massachusetts Council

PRESIDENT

Hon. Charles C. Cabot
(1943-46)

TREASURER

Allan Forbes   (1943-46)

CHAIRMAN

Philip M. Morgan   (1943-44)
William V. M. Fawcett
(1944-45)
Harold S. Fuller   (1945-46)

EXECUTIVE DIRECTOR

Albert B. Carter   (1943-45)
Kenneth M. Wilson   (1945-46)

Michigan United War Fund, Inc.

PRESIDENT

Howard C. Lawrence   (1943-44)
Albert L. Miller   (1944-46)

TREASURER

D. Hale Brake   (1943-46)

EXECUTIVE DIRECTOR

Warren D. Pierce   (1943–46)

Minnesota War Service Fund, Inc.

CHAIRMAN

J. Cameron Thomson   (1943–46)

TREASURER

Julian B. Baird   (1943–46)

EXECUTIVE DIRECTOR

Byron W. Shimp   (1943–45)
William C. Walsh   (1945–46)

Mississippi War Fund

PRESIDENT

Gov. Paul Johnson   (1943–44)
Gov. T. L. Bailey   (1944–46)

TREASURER

Buford Yerger   (1943–44)
J. D. Steitenroth   (1944–46)

CHAIRMAN

George Wallace   (1943–44)
Edmund Taylor   (1944–45)
R. C. Stovall   (1945–46)

EXECUTIVE DIRECTOR

Byron L. Burford   (1943–46)

Missouri War Chest, Inc.

PRESIDENT

Robert E. Lee Hill   (1943–45)
Hon. Norwin D. Houser
   (1945–46)

TREASURER

R. B. Price   (1943–45)
F. C. Hunt   (1945–46)

EXECUTIVE DIRECTOR

Edward D. Dail   (1943–46)

Montana War Fund

PRESIDENT

Payne Templeton   (1943–44)
L. A. Campbell   (1944–46)

TREASURER

J. G. Reitsch   (1943–46)

CHAIRMAN

Gov. Sam C. Ford   (1943–46)

EXECUTIVE DIRECTOR

L. W. Upshaw   (1943–46)

United War Fund of Nebraska, Inc.

CHAIRMAN

Thomas C. Woods   (1943–46)

TREASURER

R. E. Campbell   (1943–46)

EXECUTIVE DIRECTOR

Walter F. Roberts   (1943–46)

Italics: Deceased

NWF, Inc.—Nevada Division

PRESIDENT

Hon. Morley Griswold   (1943-46)

EXECUTIVE DIRECTOR

Charles L. Duffer   (1943-44)
George A. Clark   (1944-46)

TREASURER

Harold Gorman   (1943-46)

New Hampshire War Chest, Inc.

PRESIDENT

Frank J. Sulloway   (1943-44)
Robert P. Booth   (1944-45)
John P. Carleton   (1945-46)

TREASURER

Edgar C. Hirst   (1943-44)
H. Ellis Straw   (1944-46)

EXECUTIVE DIRECTOR

F. Donald Gordon   (1943-44)
Orlo F. King   (1944-45)
Merton J. Stickel   (1945-46)

NWF—New Jersey Division, Inc.

PRESIDENT

Franklin D'Olier   (1943-46)

TREASURER

Robert Cowan   (1943-46)

CHAIRMAN

Gill Robb Wilson   (1945-46)

EXECUTIVE DIRECTOR

Guy Codding   (1943-44)
H. A. Waldkoenig   (1944-46)

NWF—New Mexico Committee

PRESIDENT

Hon. James M. Murray, Sr.
(1943-44)
Hon. Thomas J. Mabry
(1944-46)

TREASURER

Guy Shephard   (1943-44)
R. L. Ormsbee   (1944-46)

EXECUTIVE DIRECTOR

Frank J. McCarthy   (1943-46)

New York United War Fund, Inc.   (Up-state)

PRESIDENT

Stewart F. Hancock   (1943-46)

TREASURER

Crandall Melvin   (1943-46)

EXECUTIVE DIRECTOR

John F. Chambers   (1943-46)

Italics: Deceased

New York National War Fund   (New York City)

PRESIDENT   TREASURER

Lindsay Bradford (1943–46)   H. Donald Campbell (1943–46)

CHAIRMAN   EXECUTIVE DIRECTOR

Emil Schram (1943–44)   Percival Dodge (1943–45)
Richard W. Lawrence (1944–45)   Virgil Martin (1945–46)
Carl Whitmore (1945–46)

National War Fund of Nassau County

CHAIRMAN   TREASURER

Hon. Elvin N. Edwards   Hon. Harry L. Hedger
(1943–46)   (1943–46)

CO-CHAIRMAN   EXECUTIVE DIRECTOR

Mrs. Preston Davie (1944–46)   C. A. Tevebaugh (1943–46)

National War Fund of Suffolk County

CHAIRMAN   TREASURER

Fred J. Munder (1943–46)   Mrs. Chas. S. Robertson
(1943–46)

EXECUTIVE DIRECTOR
C. A. Tevebaugh (1943–46)

National War Fund, Westchester County

CHAIRMAN   TREASURER

Hon. George W. Smyth   J. Marshall Perley (1943–46)
(1943–46)

EXECUTIVE DIRECTOR
A. R. Williams (1943–46)

United War Fund of North Carolina

CHAIRMAN   TREASURER

Robert M. Hanes (1943–44)   J. C. B. Ehringhaus (1943–44)
Major L. P. McLendon (1944–45)   T. L. Carroll (1944–45)
Victor S. Bryant (1945–46)   Gurney P. Hood (1945–46)

EXECUTIVE DIRECTOR
Thomas L. Carroll (1943–44)
Chester A. Kerr (1944–46)

Italics: Deceased

North Dakota War Chest, Inc.

PRESIDENT
H. A. Brandes (1943–46)

TREASURER
Carl Anderson (1943–44)
Otto Krueger (1944–45)
H. W. Swenson (1945–46)

EXECUTIVE SECRETARY
Thomas C. Brown (1943–46)

NWF—Ohio Division, Inc.

PRESIDENT
Charles F. Kennedy (1943–46)

TREASURER
Joseph W. Fichter (1943–44)
Perry L. Green (1944–46)

EXECUTIVE DIRECTOR
Robert V. Clapp (1943–45)
W. Walker Wyatt (1945–46)

United War Chest of Oklahoma

PRESIDENT
Carl C. Magee (1943–46)

TREASURER
Hugh L. Harrell (1943–46)

EXECUTIVE DIRECTOR
Walter B. Schoggen (1943–44)
Kelly E. DeBusk (1944–46)

Oregon War Chest, Inc.

PRESIDENT
Hon. Chas. A. Sprague
(1943–46)

TREASURER
J. J. Gard (1943–46)

EXECUTIVE DIRECTOR
Irl S. McSherry (1943–46)

Pennsylvania War Fund, Inc.

PRESIDENT
William P. Witherow (1943–46)

TREASURER
Donald McCormick (1943–45)
Harper W. Spong (1945–46)

CHAIRMAN
Ralph E. Weeks (1943–46)

EXECUTIVE DIRECTOR
Wilbur F. Maxwell (1943–46)

Italics: Deceased

Rhode Island United War Fund, Inc.

PRESIDENT   TREASURER
Henry M. Wriston   (1943–46)   Ernest Clayton   (1943–46)

CHAIRMAN   EXECUTIVE DIRECTOR
Rupert C. Thompson, Jr.   Robert O. Loosley   (1943–46)
(1943–44)
Raymond H. Trott   (1944–46)

South Carolina State War Fund

CHAIRMAN   TREASURER
Hon. Richard M. Jefferies   Angus E. Bird   (1943–46)
(1943–46)

EXECUTIVE DIRECTOR
Samuel B. Moyle   (1943–46)

NWF—South Dakota Committee

CHAIRMAN   TREASURER
Dr. V. A. Lowry   (1943–46)   A. M. Parker   (1943–46)

EXECUTIVE DIRECTOR
George F. Warner   (1943–44)
R. S. Wallace   (1944–46)

National War Fund in Tennessee, Inc.

PRESIDENT   TREASURER
Col. T. Walker Lewis   (1943–46)   L. E. Wittenberg   (1943–46)

CHAIRMAN   EXECUTIVE DIRECTOR
W. Dudley Gale   (1943–46)   Earle L. Whittington   (1943–46)

United War Chest of Texas, Inc.

PRESIDENT   TREASURER
George A. Butler   (1943–44)   James Clayton   (1943–44)
Hon. Ben H. Powell   (1944–46)   L. D. Williams   (1944–46)

EXECUTIVE DIRECTOR
Wayland D. Towner   (1943–46)

United War Fund of Utah

PRESIDENT   TREASURER
Hon. Earl J. Glade   (1943–46)   E. O. Howard   (1943–46)

EXECUTIVE DIRECTOR
Herbert M. Schiller   (1943–46)

Vermont War Chest, Inc.

PRESIDENT

Ralph E. Flanders (1943-44)
Hon. William H. Wills
(1944-46)

TREASURER

Earl S. Wright (1943-46)

CHAIRMAN

Esme A. C. Smith (1943-46)

EXECUTIVE DIRECTOR

William E. Ashton (1943-46)

Virginia War Fund, Inc.

PRESIDENT

Homer L. Ferguson (1943-44)
W. Tayloe Murphy (1944-46)

TREASURER

H. Hiter Harris (1943-46)

EXECUTIVE SECRETARY

J. W. Phillips (1943-44)
J. Linwood Rice (1944-46)

Washington State War Fund, Inc.

PRESIDENT

W. Walter Williams (1943-44)
Philip S. Brooke (1944-45)
Henry R. Kruse (1945-46)

TREASURER

J. E. Ferris (1943-44)
J. M. Tedford (1944-45)
Henry J. Dolling (1945-46)

EXECUTIVE DIRECTOR

George N. Porter (1943-46)

West Virginia State War Fund Committee

CHAIRMAN

R. E. Talbot (1943-44)
Carl O. Schmidt (1944-45)
Buford C. Tynes (1945-46)

TREASURER

Mason Crickard (1943-46)

EXECUTIVE DIRECTOR

Victor Lecoq (1943-44)
William V. Mueller (1944-46)

Wisconsin War Fund, Inc.

PRESIDENT

Frank A. Ross (1943-46)

TREASURER

Rex Reeder (1943-46)

CHAIRMAN

Robert L. Reisinger (1943-46)

Italics: Deceased

EXECUTIVE DIRECTOR
Leonard E. Blackmer   (1943–46)

NWF—Wyoming Committee

PRESIDENT   TREASURER
W. O. Wilson   (1943–44)   Ralph Barton   (1944–46)
E. J. Schulte   (1944–46)

EXECUTIVE DIRECTOR
Walter Hopkins   (1944–46)

National War Relief Fund—Alaska Division

CHAIRMAN   TREASURER
Mrs. John L. McCormick   James McNaughton   (1943–46)
    (1943–46)

Isthmian National War Fund   (Canal Zone)

CHAIRMAN   TREASURER
C. M. Lupfer   (1943–46)   M. B. Huff   (1943–44)
                                                      J. H. Smith   (1944–45)
                                                      J. W. Greene   (1944–46)

Hawaii Committee of the National War Fund

CHAIRMAN   TREASURER
P. E. Spalding   (1943–46)   Hawaiian Trust Co., Ltd.
                                                      (1943–46)

EXECUTIVE DIRECTOR
Arthur H. Eyles, III   (1943–46)

National War Fund—Puerto Rico Division

CHAIRMAN   TREASURER
Jose M. Gallardo   (1944–46)   Rafael Carrion, Sr.   (1945–46)

NWF—Virgin Islands Division

PRESIDENT   TREASURER
Hon. Charles Harwood   Louis Shulterbrandt   (1944–46)
    (1944–46)

CHAIRMAN
Morris F. de Castro   (1944–46)

INDEX

181